The Art Of Street Art and Graffiti Coloring Book For Adults

GRAFFITI

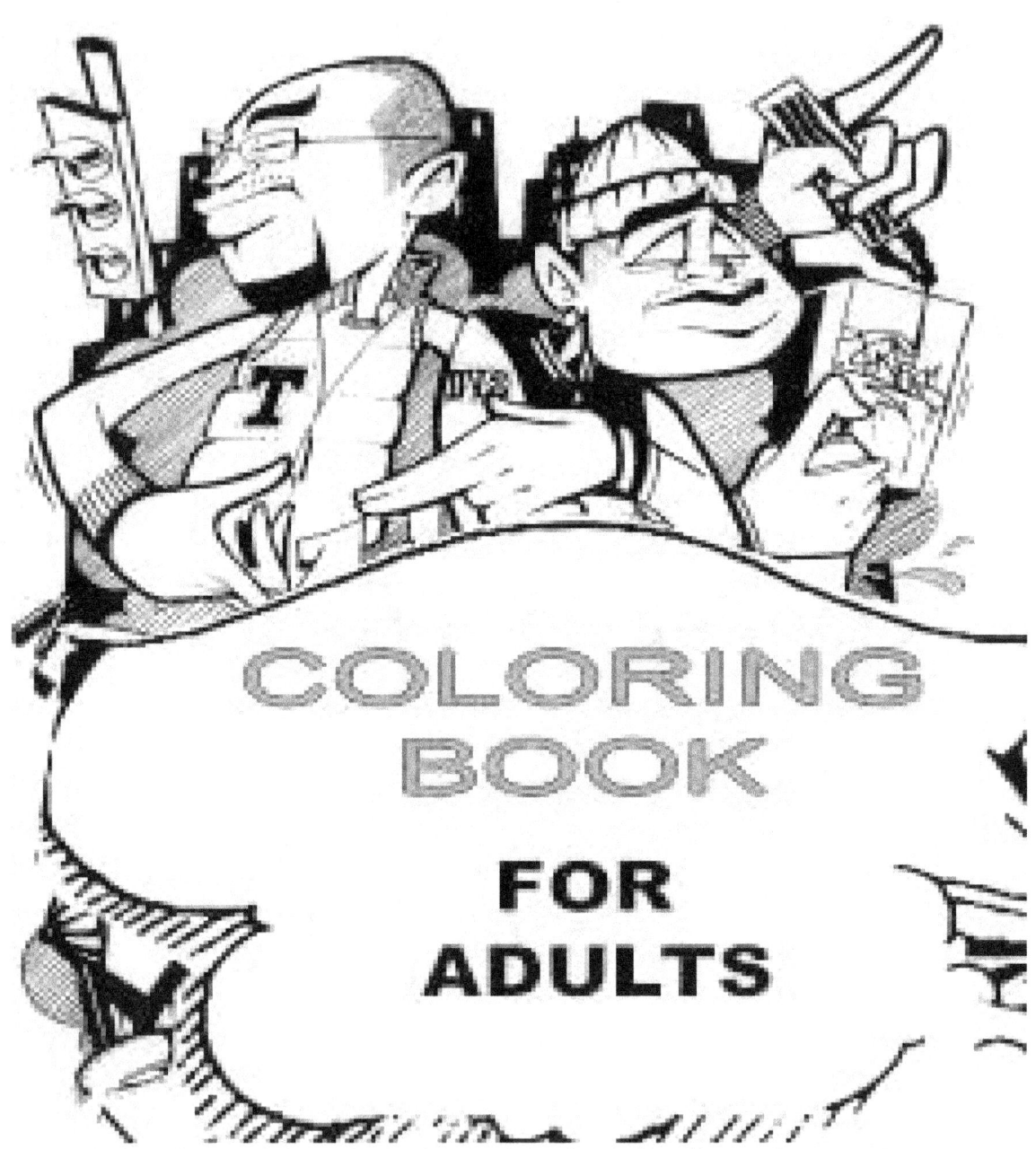

Copyright © 2020
All rights reserved. No part of this publication may be copied, Reproduced in any format, by any means, electronic or otherwise,
Without prior consent from the copyright owner and publisher of this book

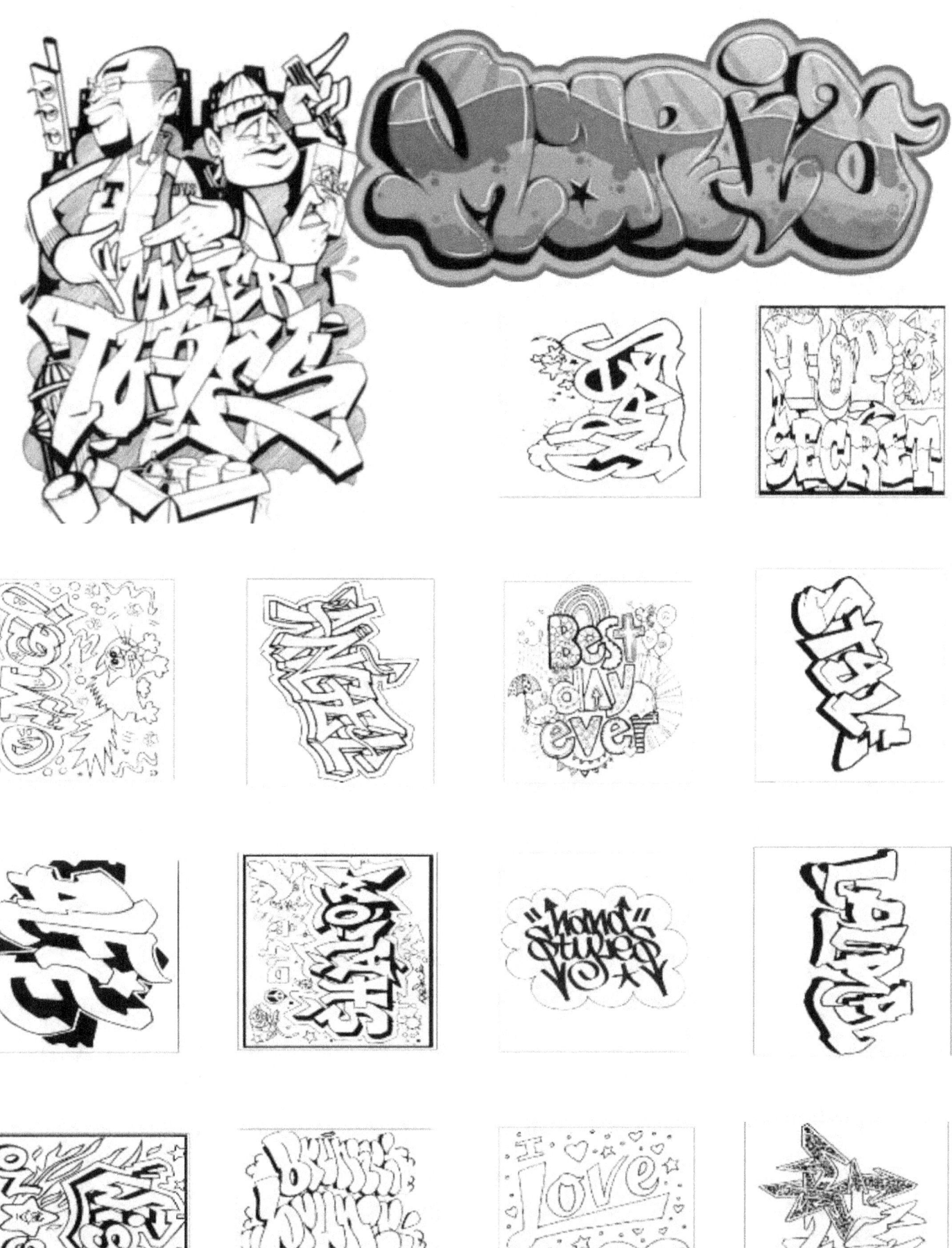

TEST COLOR PAGE
CHECK HOW YOUR COLORS SHOW OUR PAPER HERE

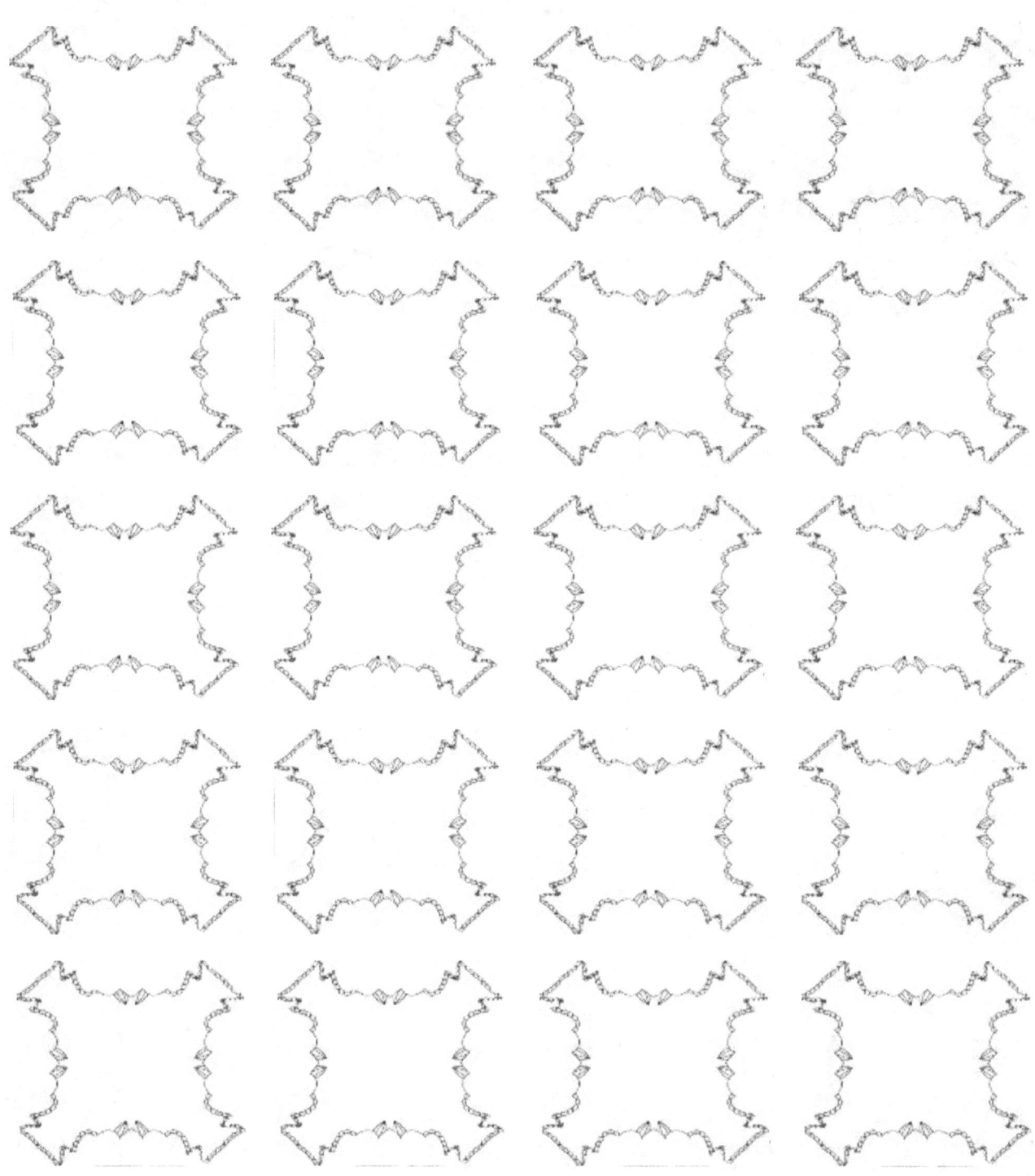

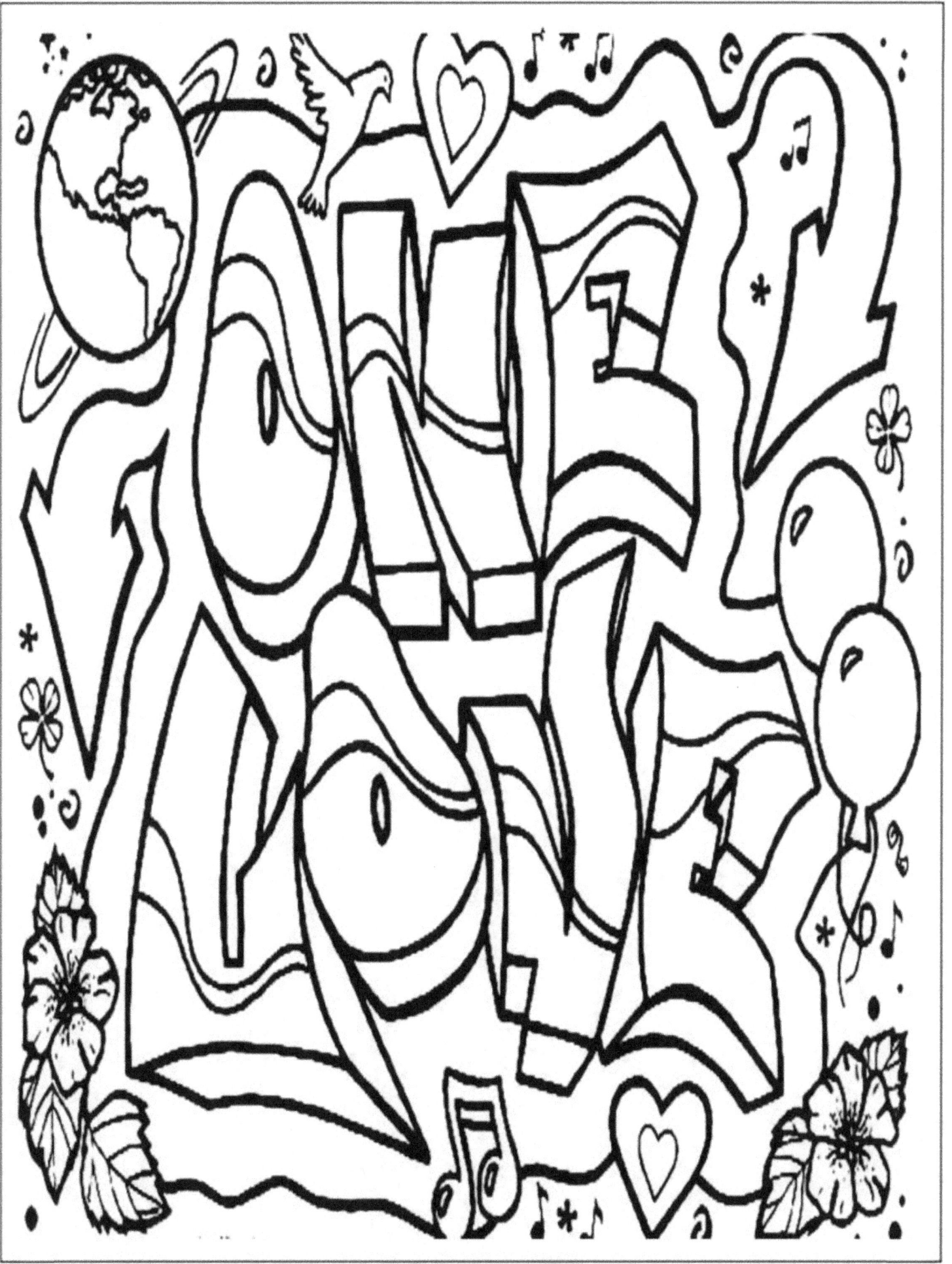

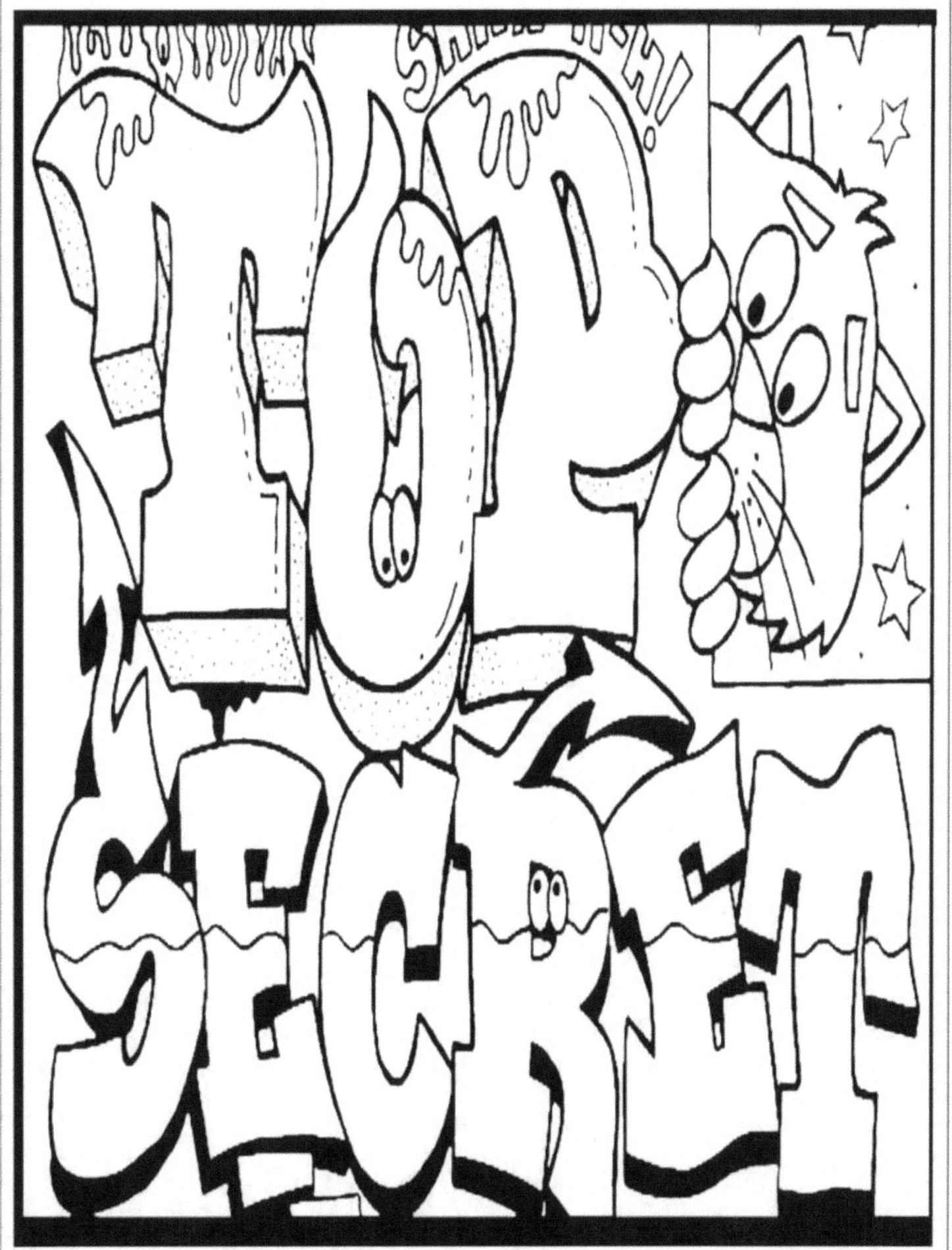

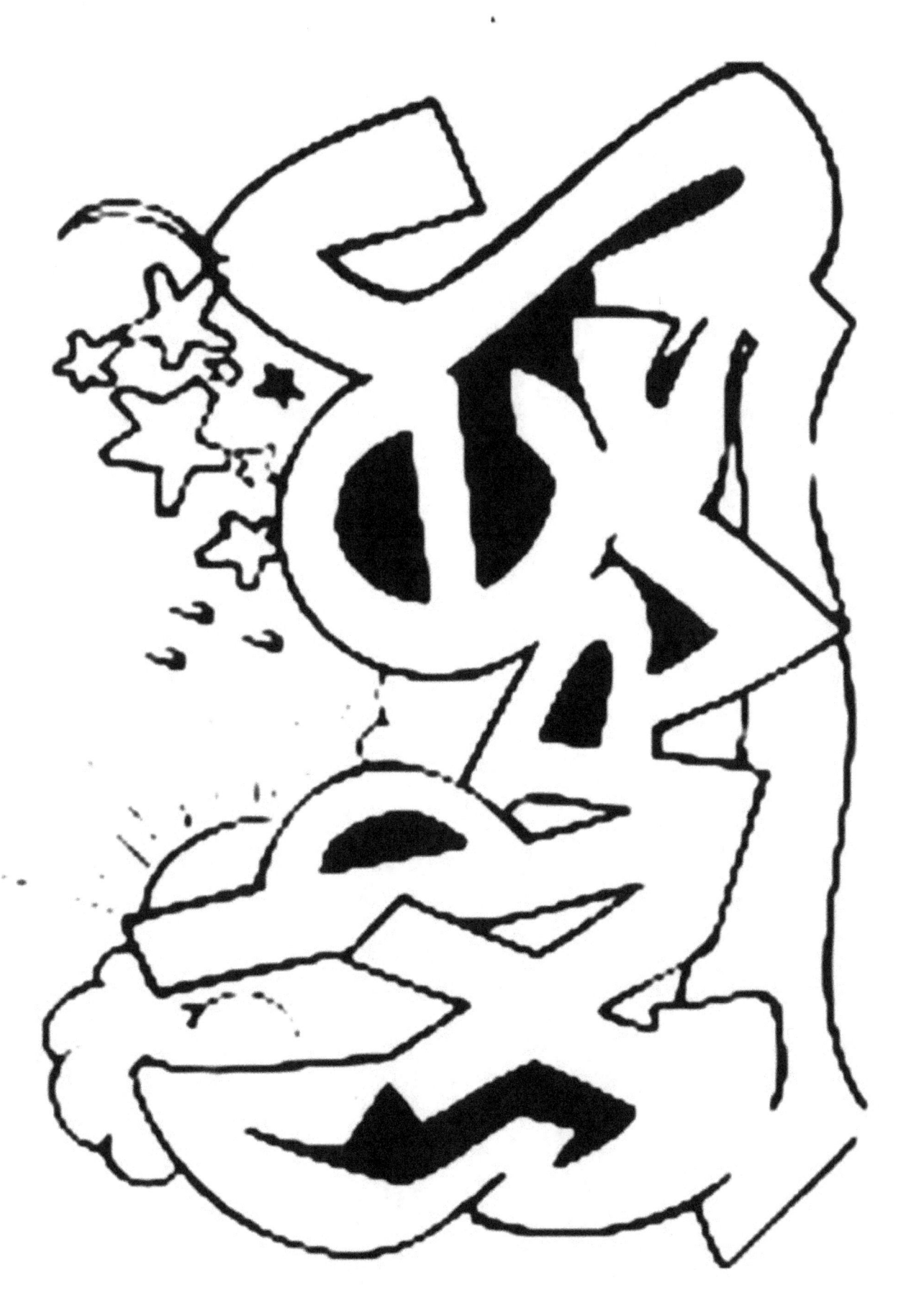

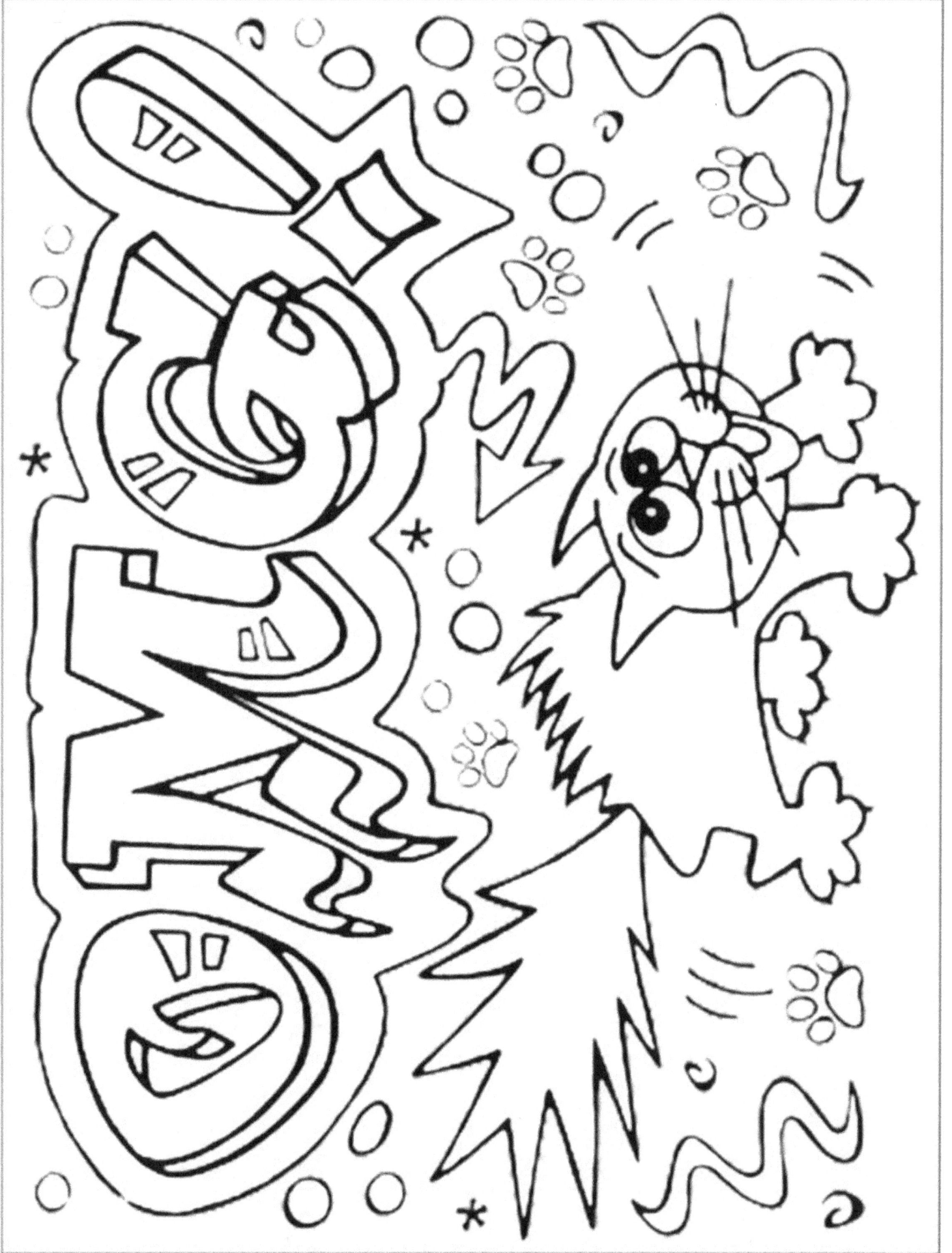

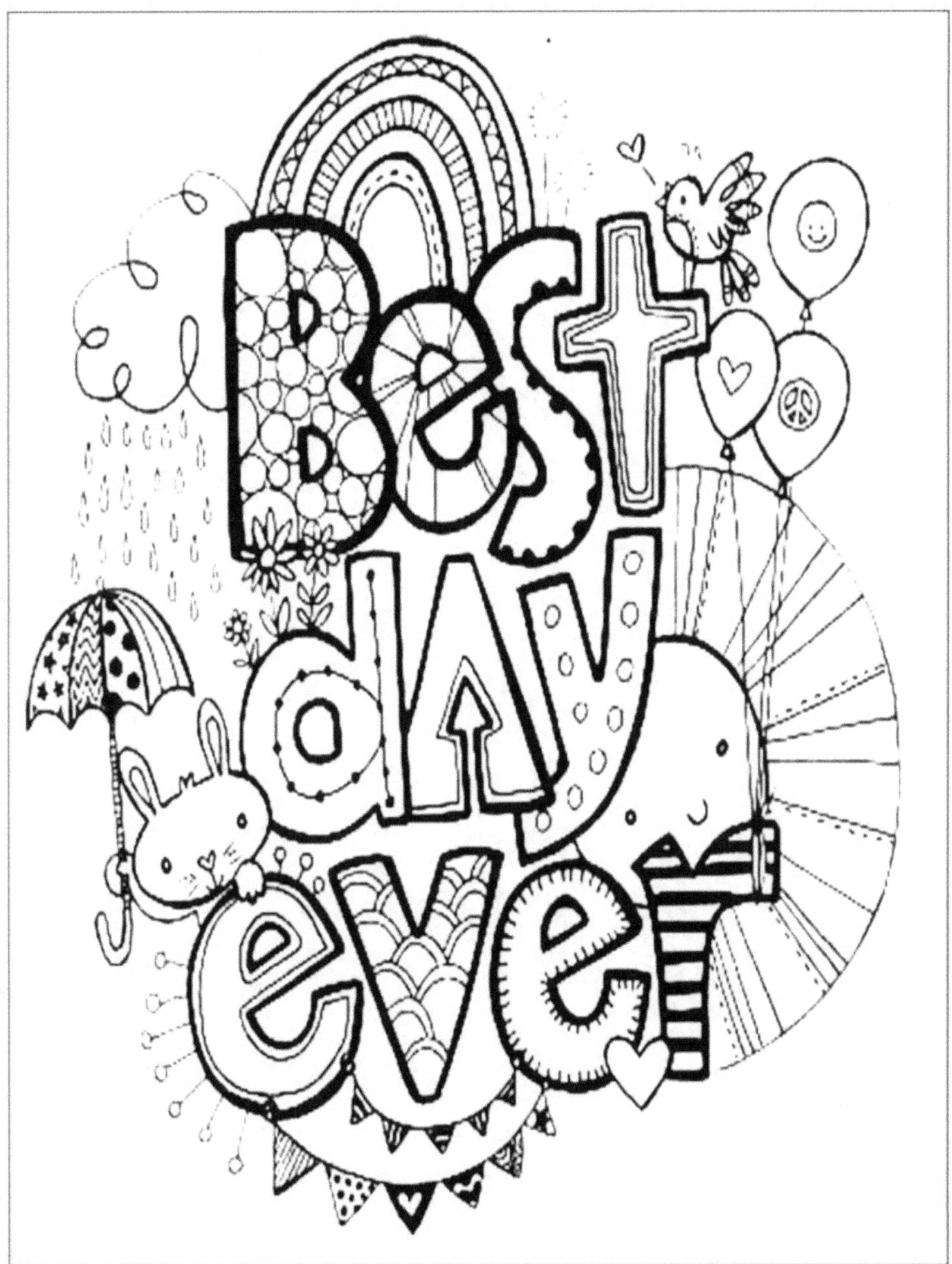

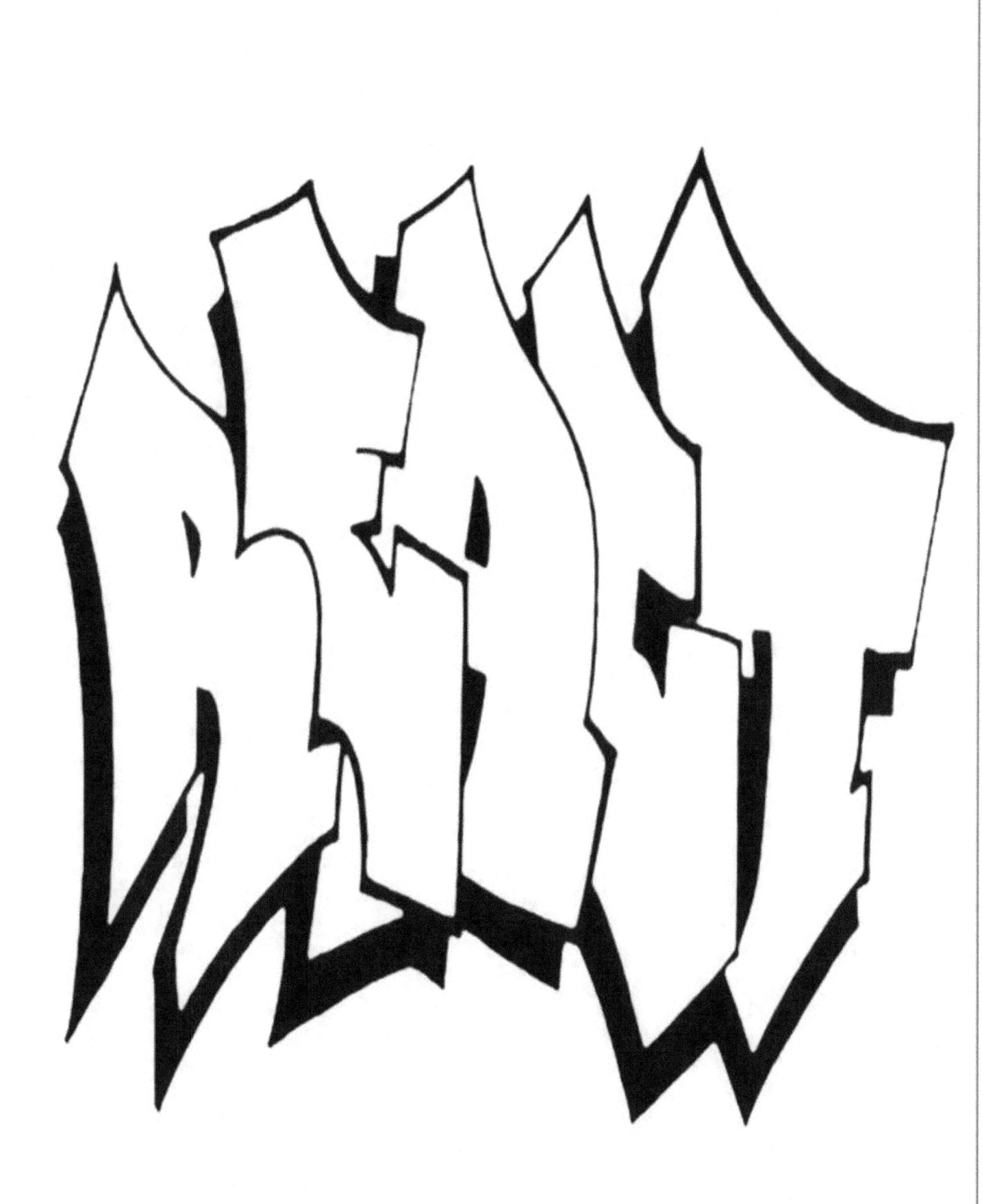

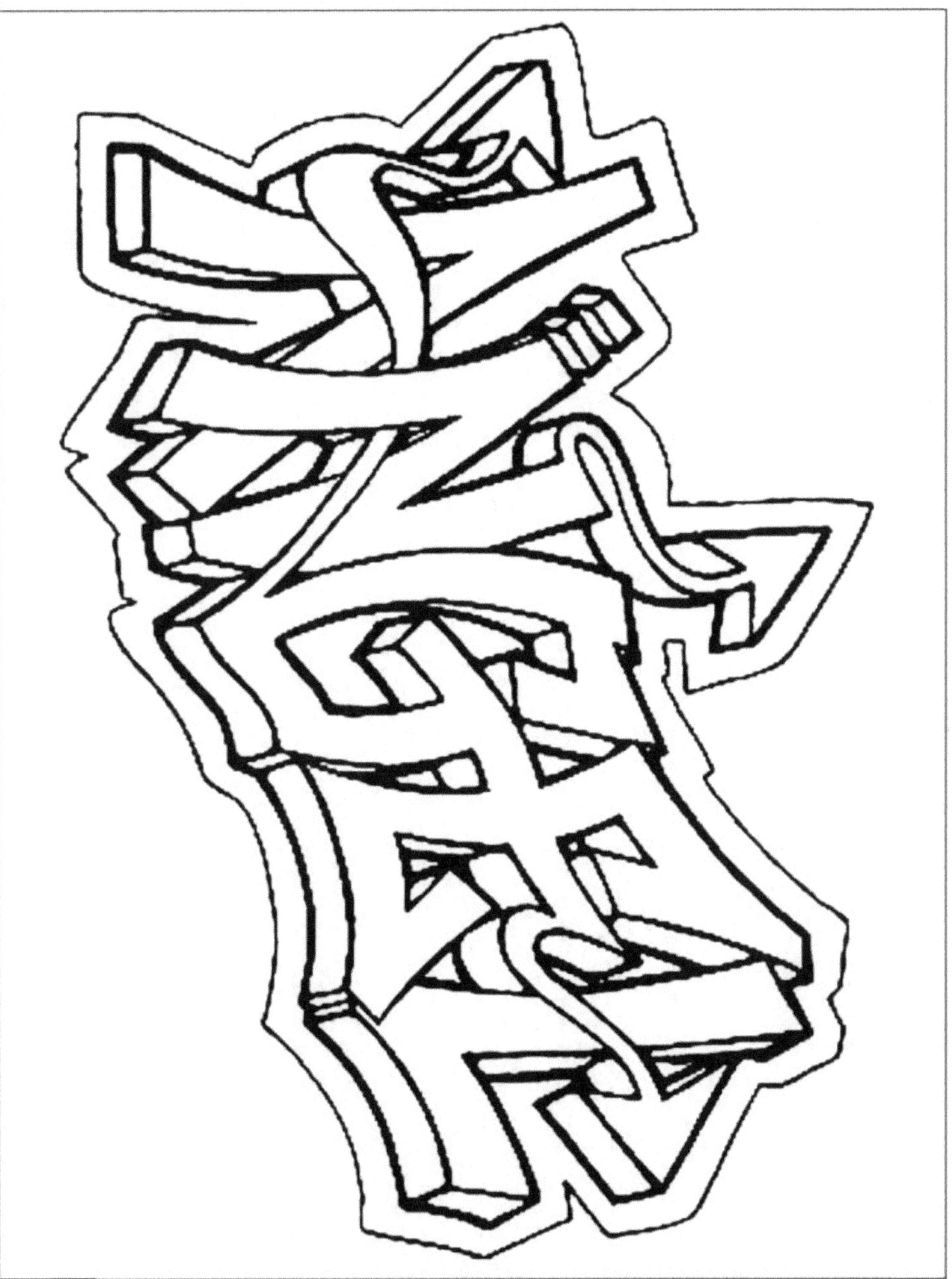

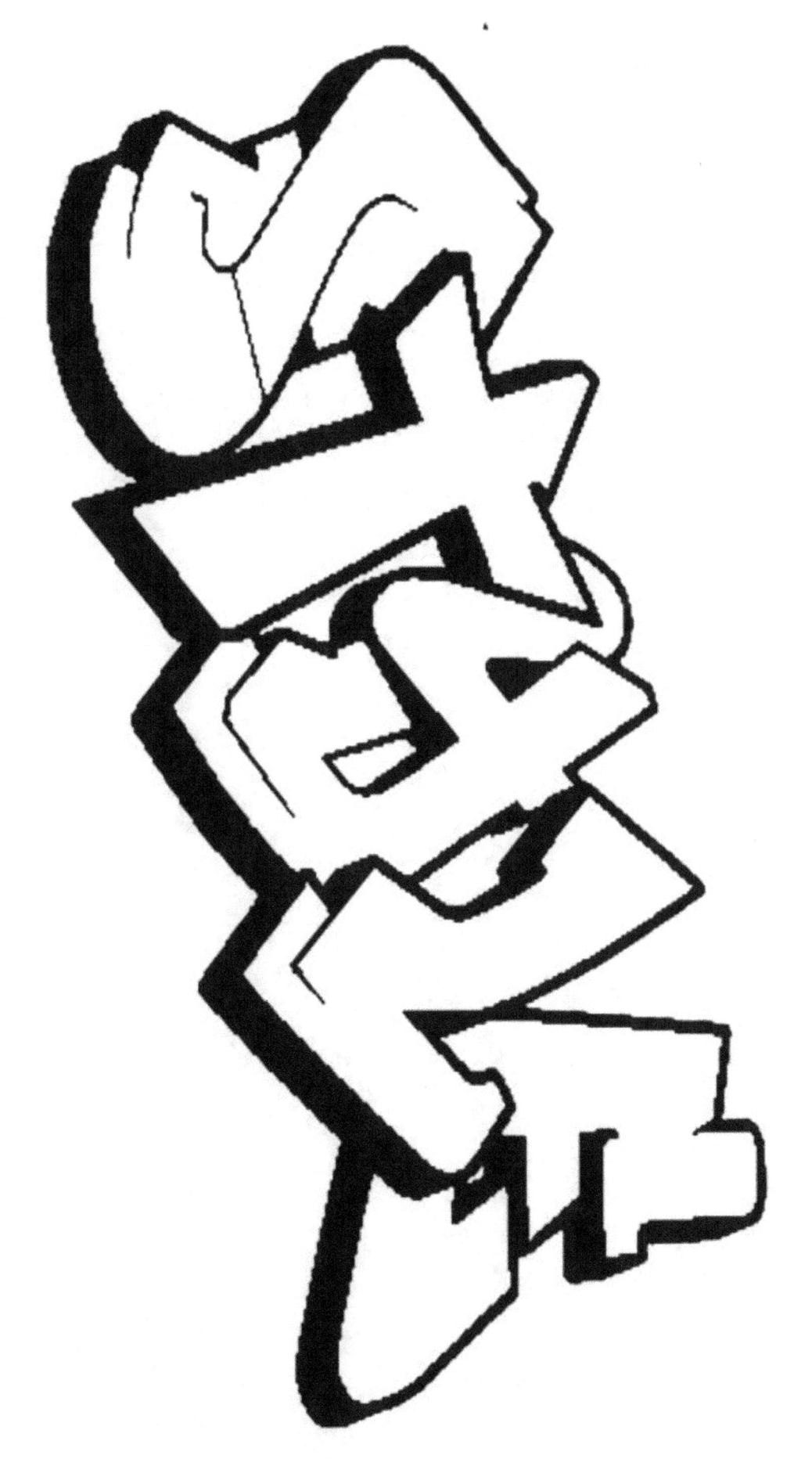

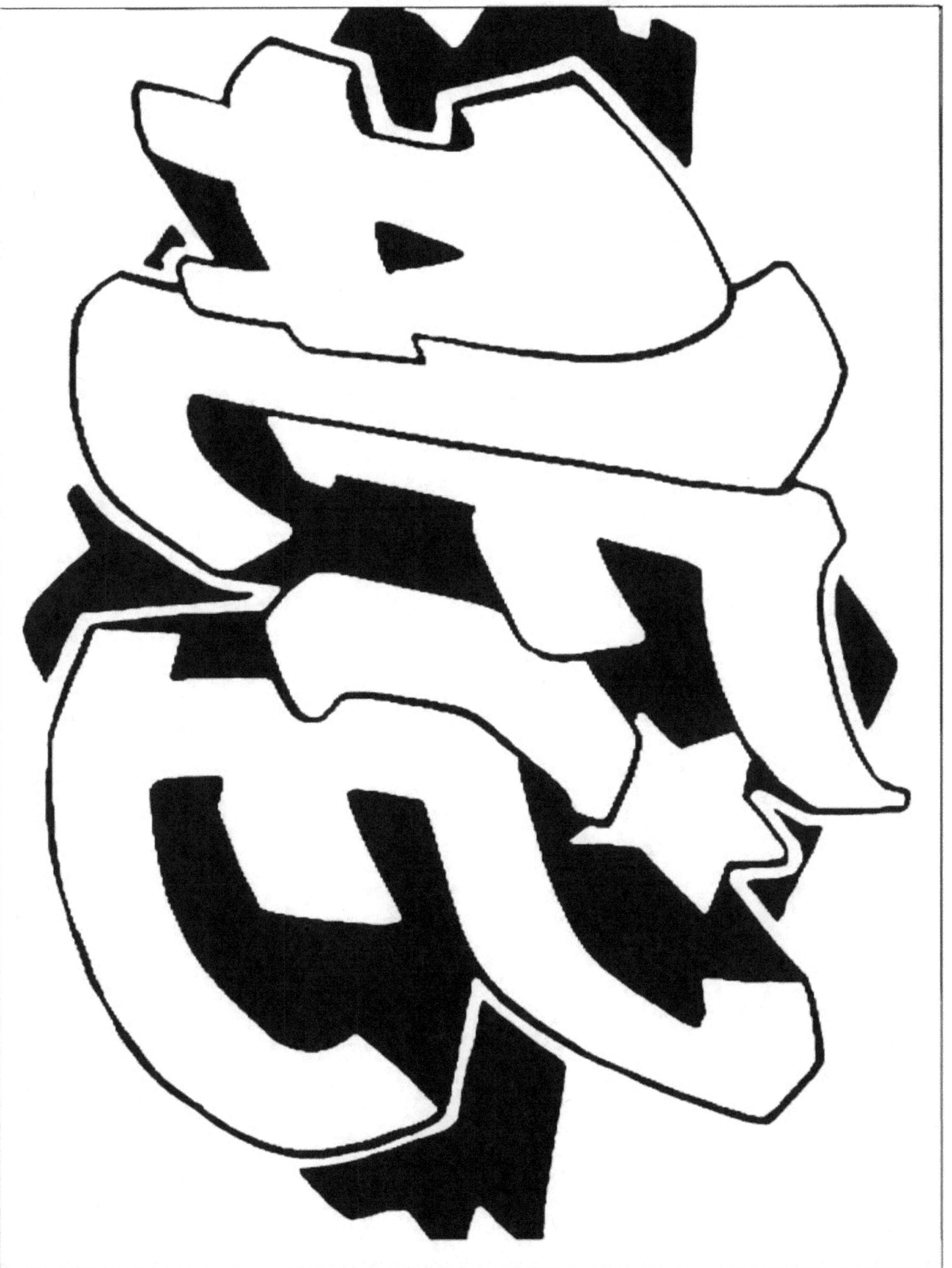

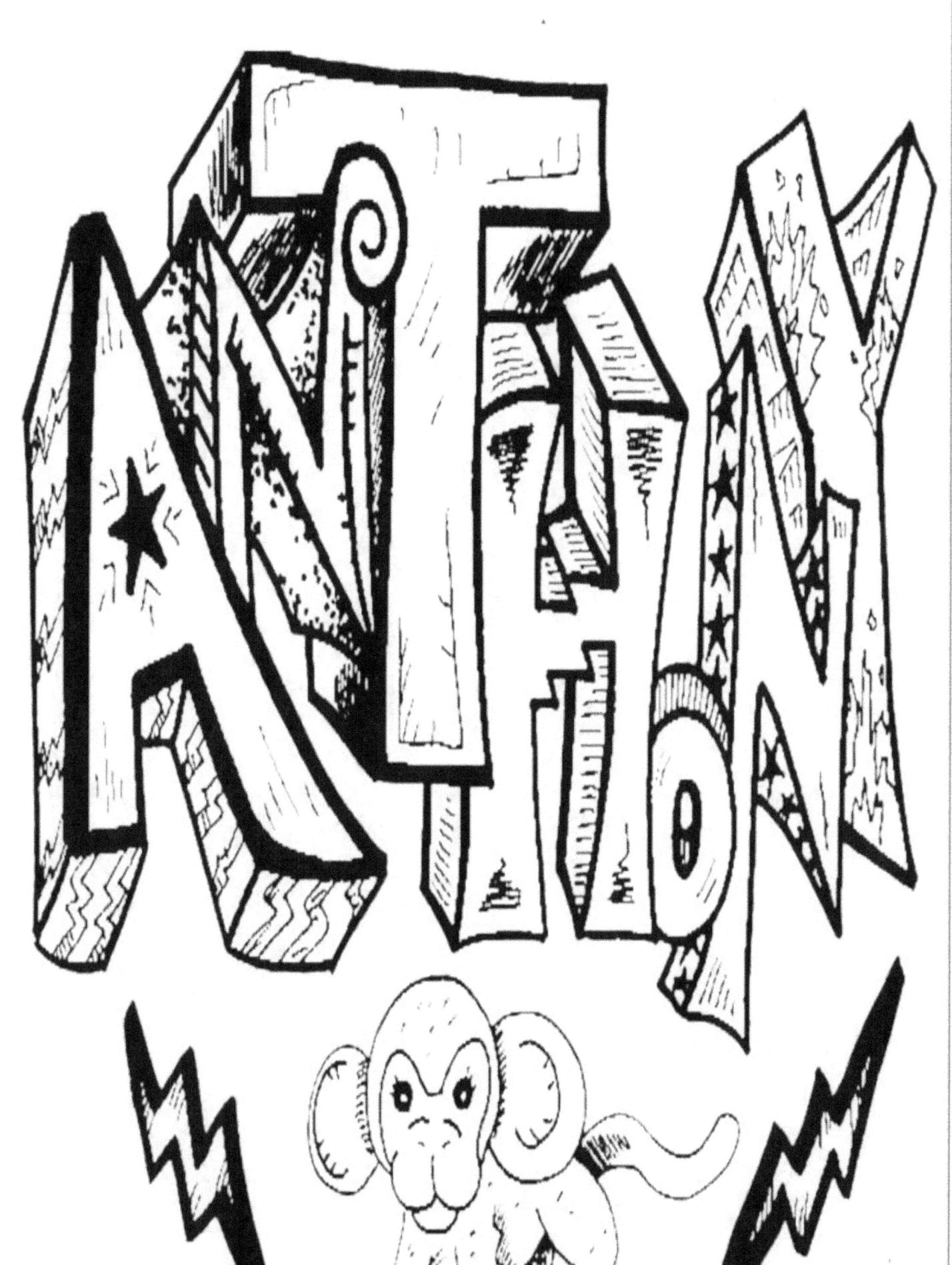

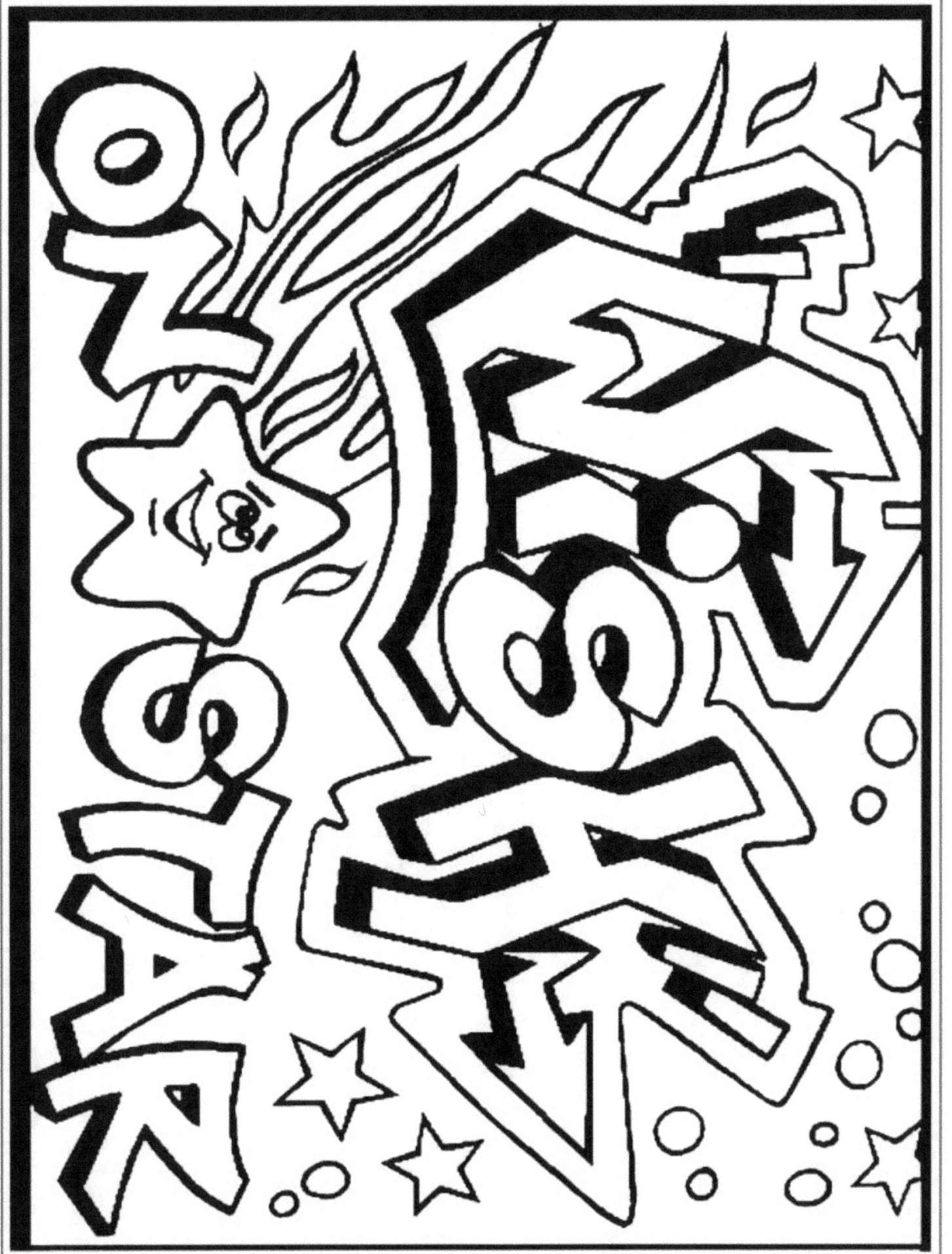

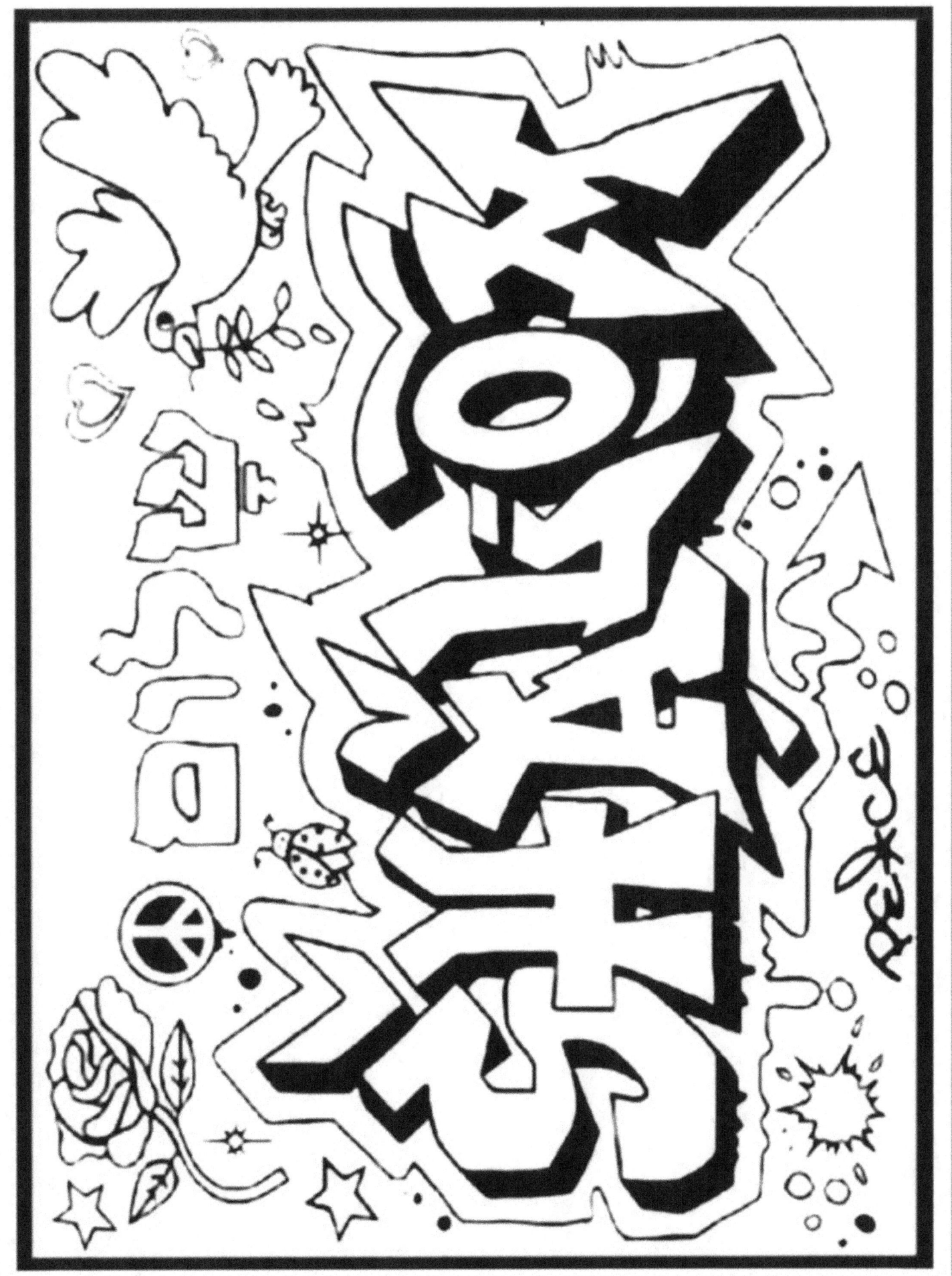

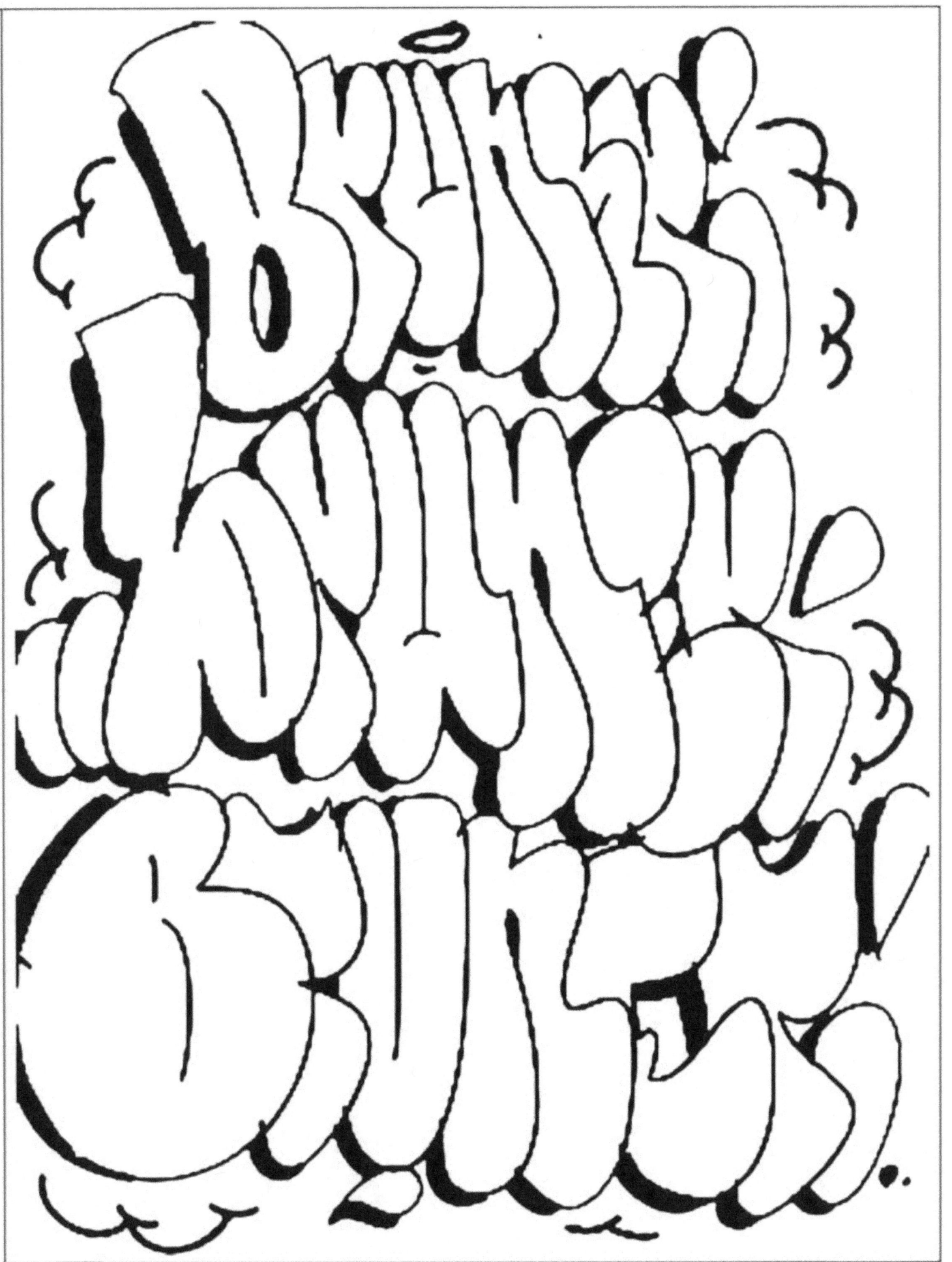

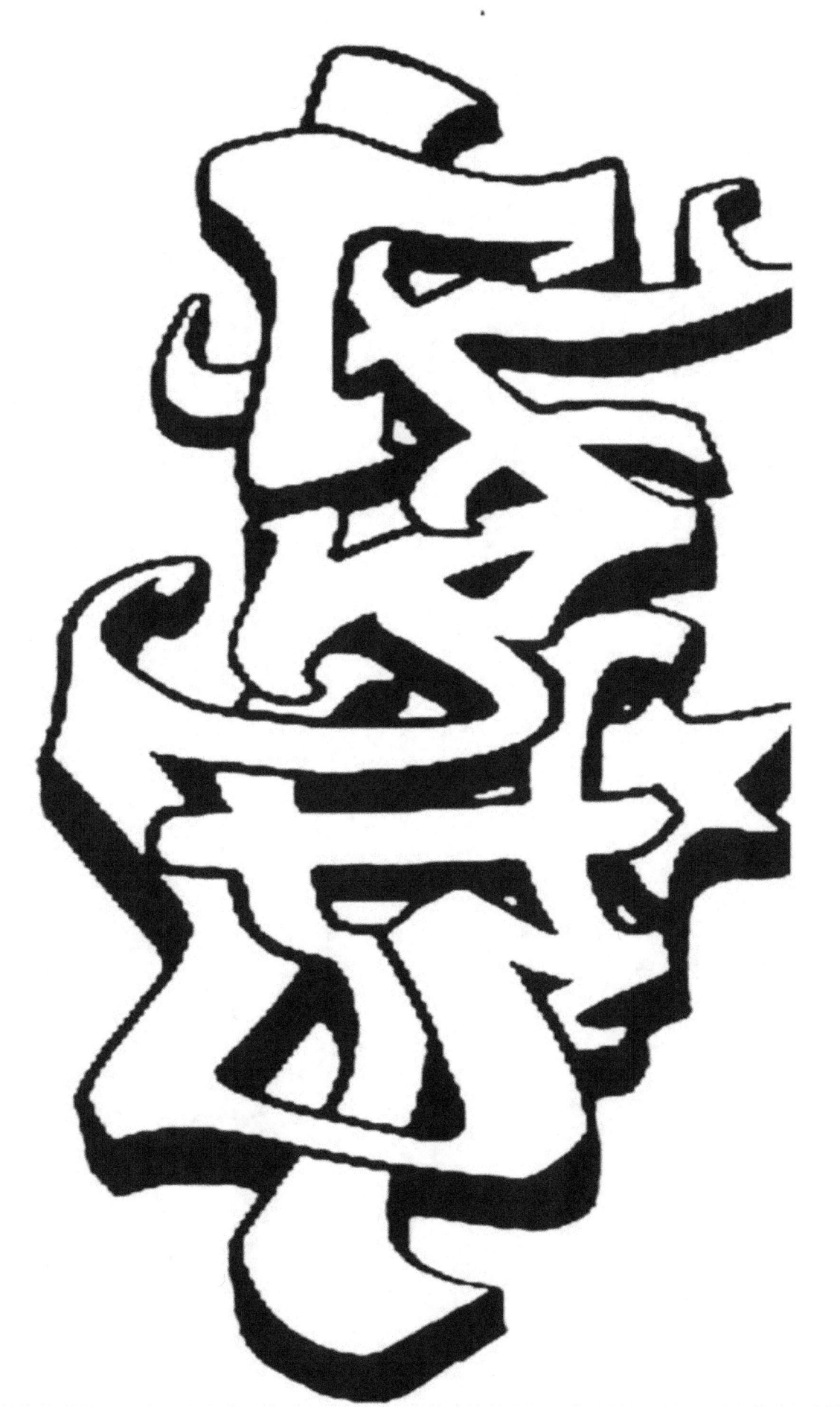

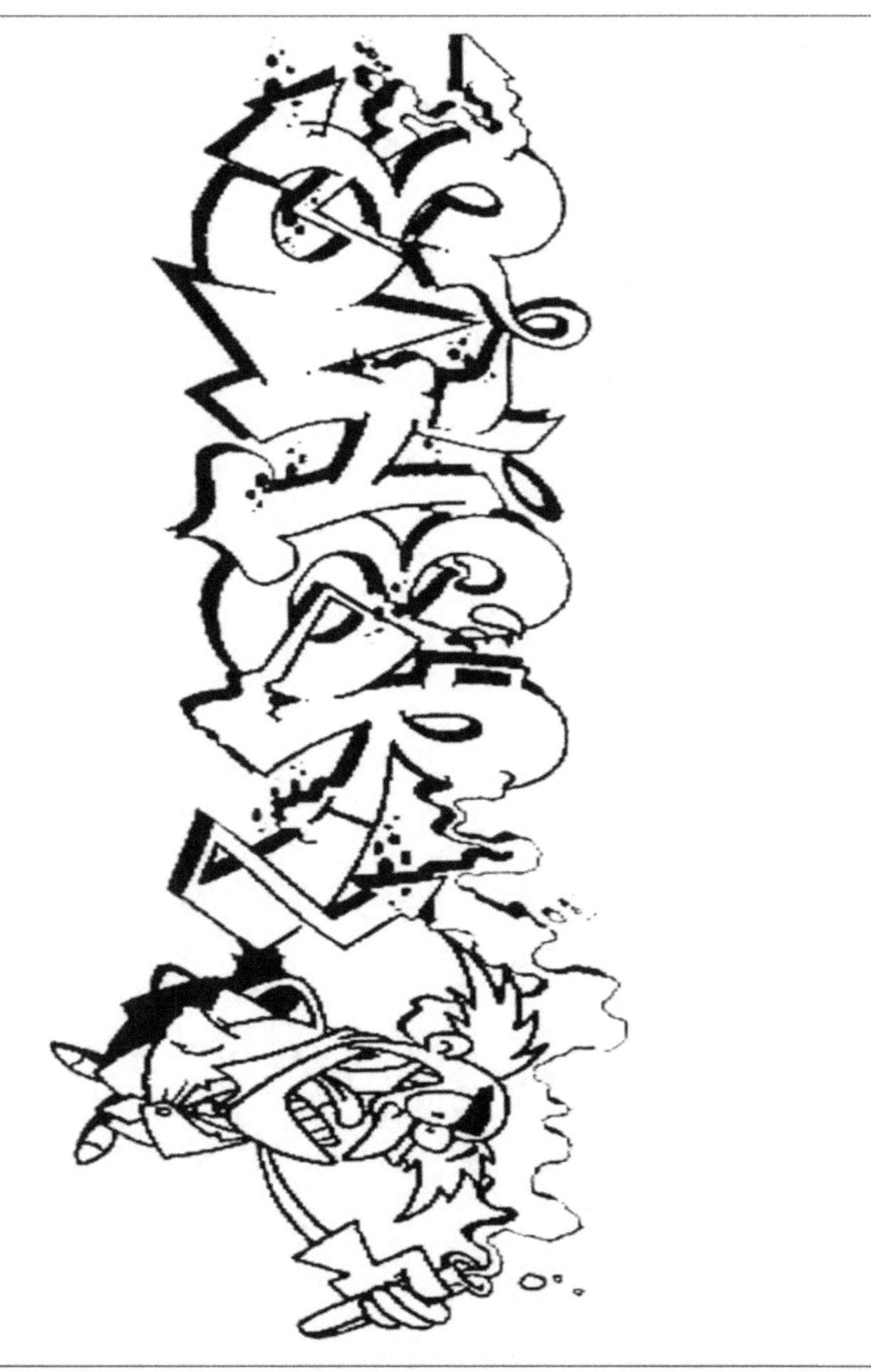

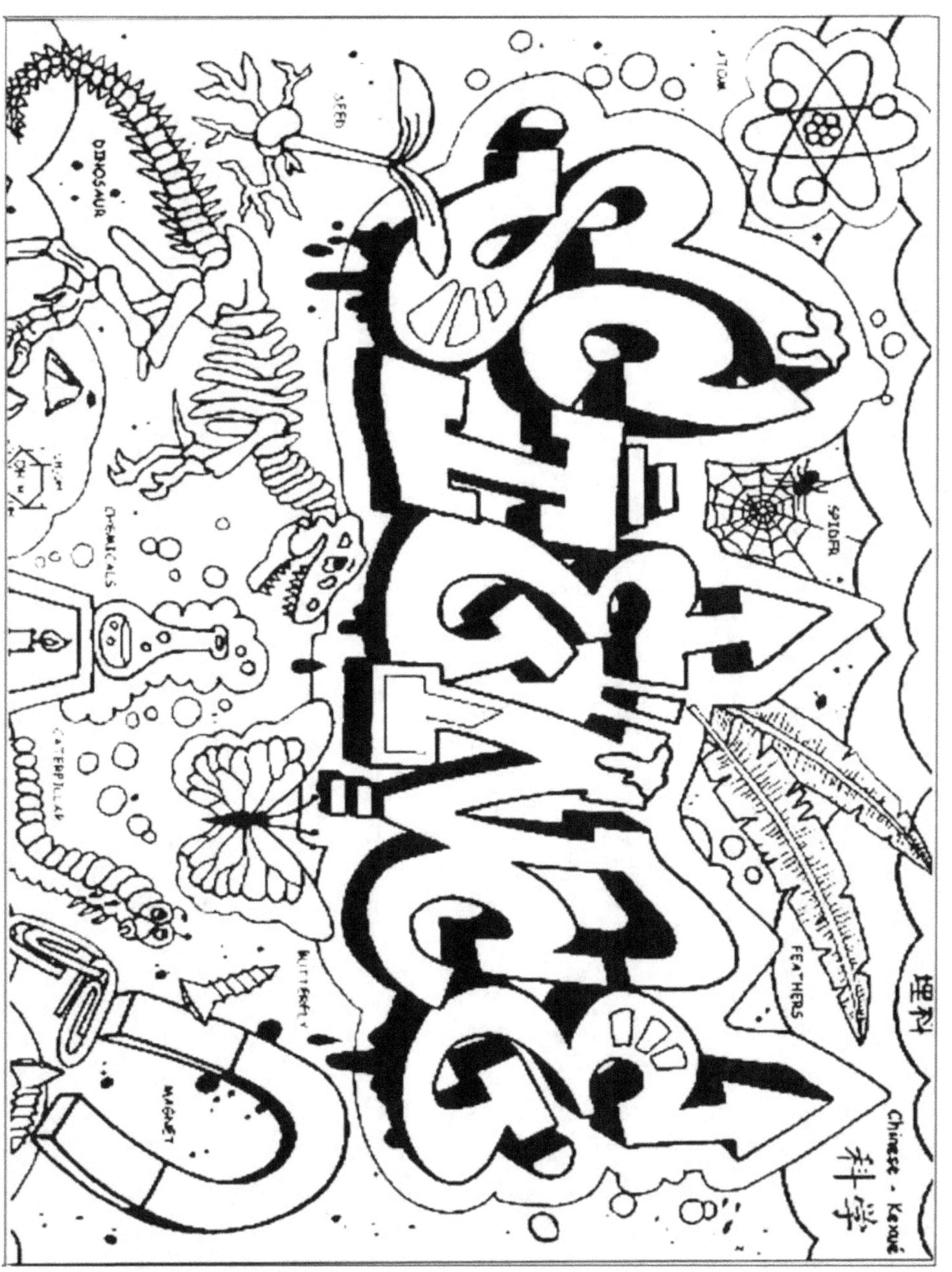

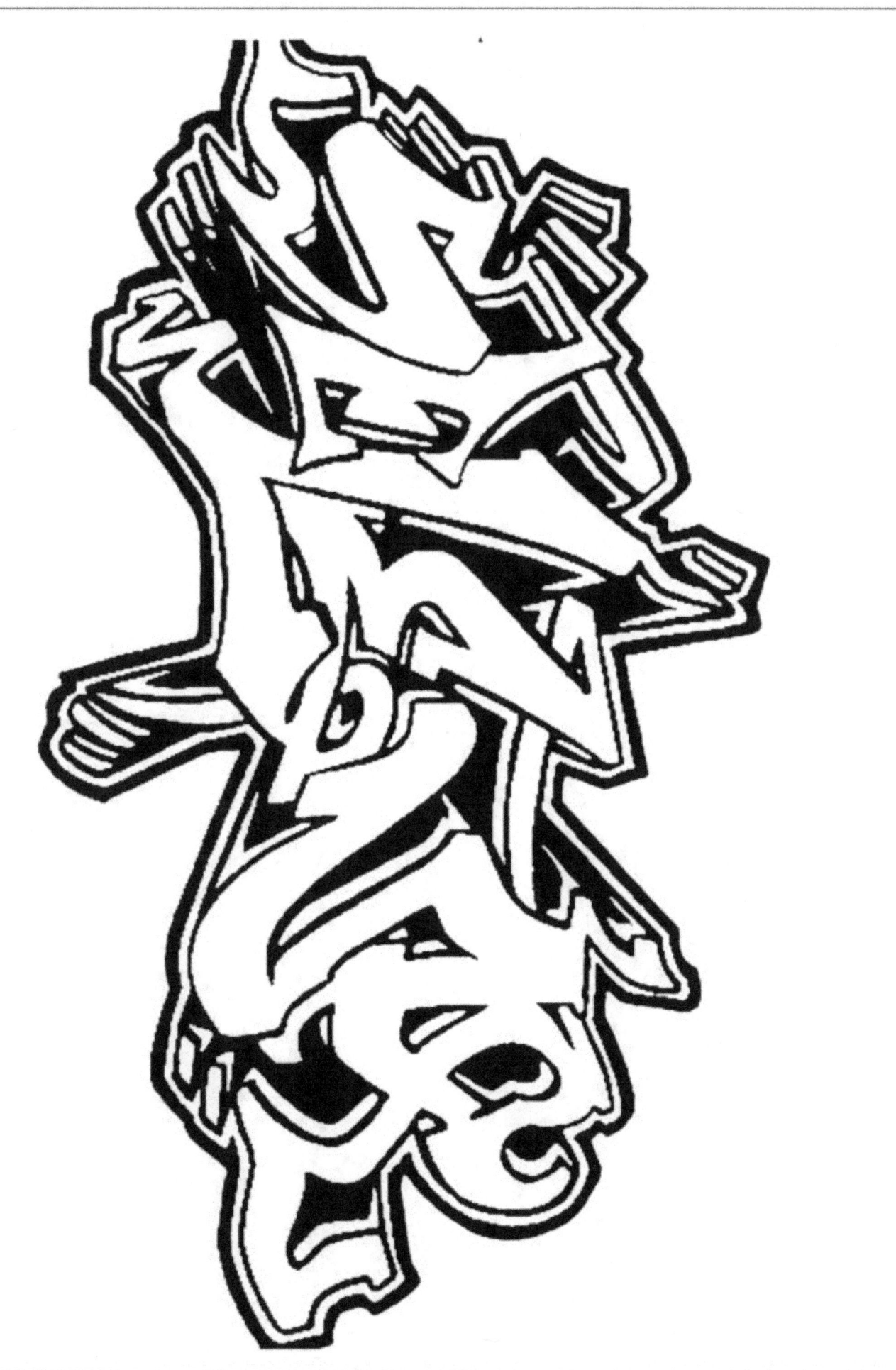

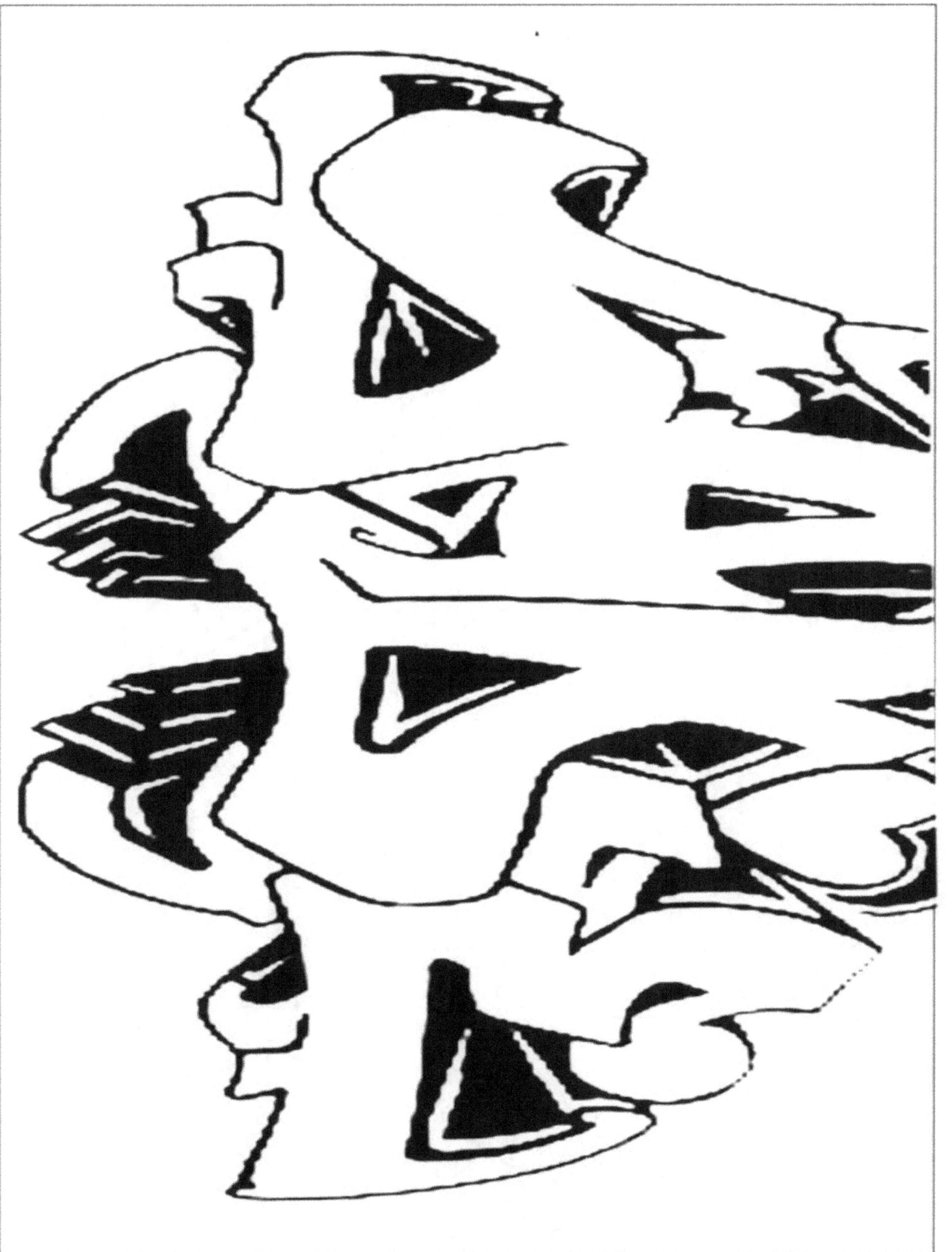

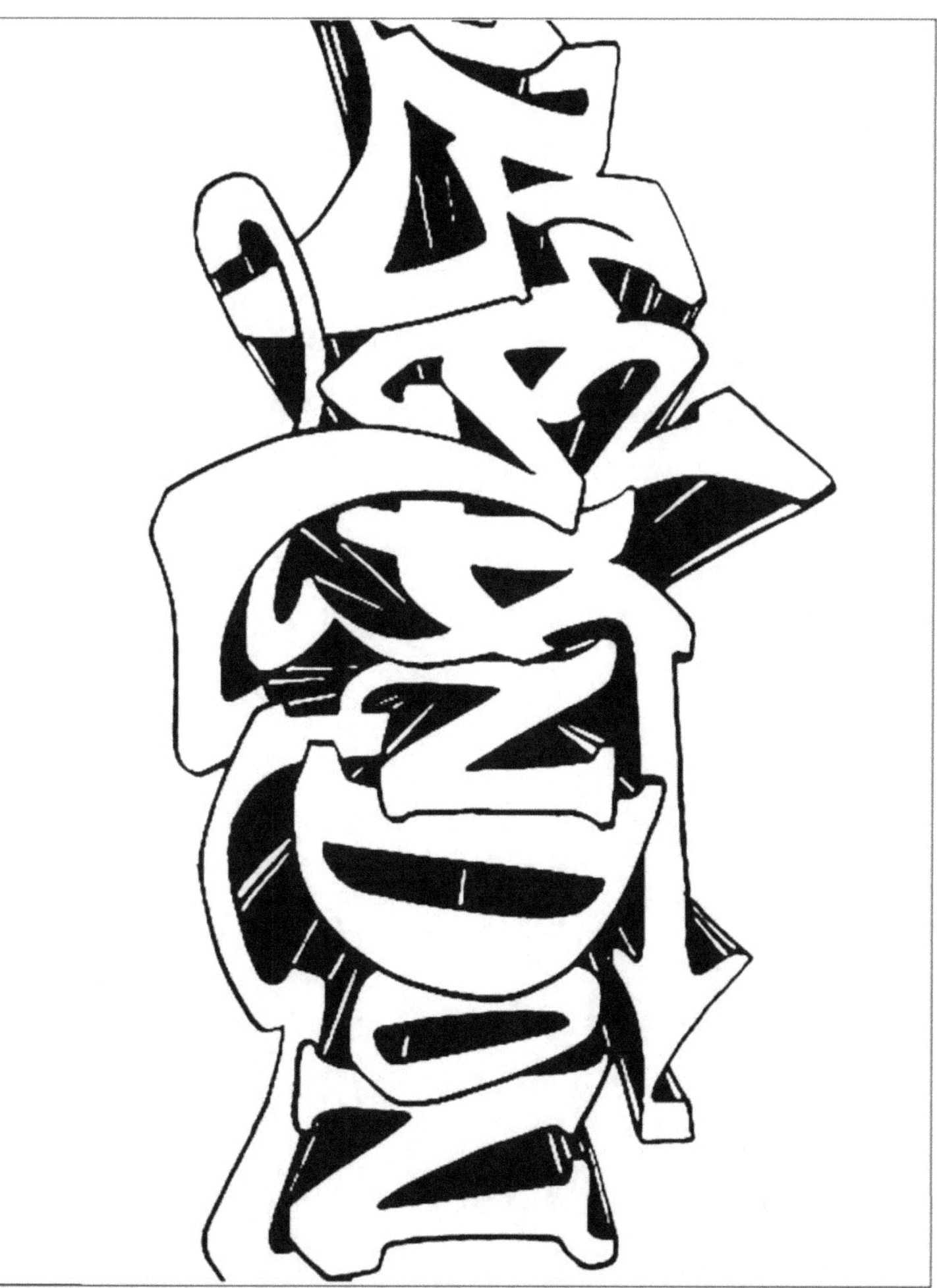

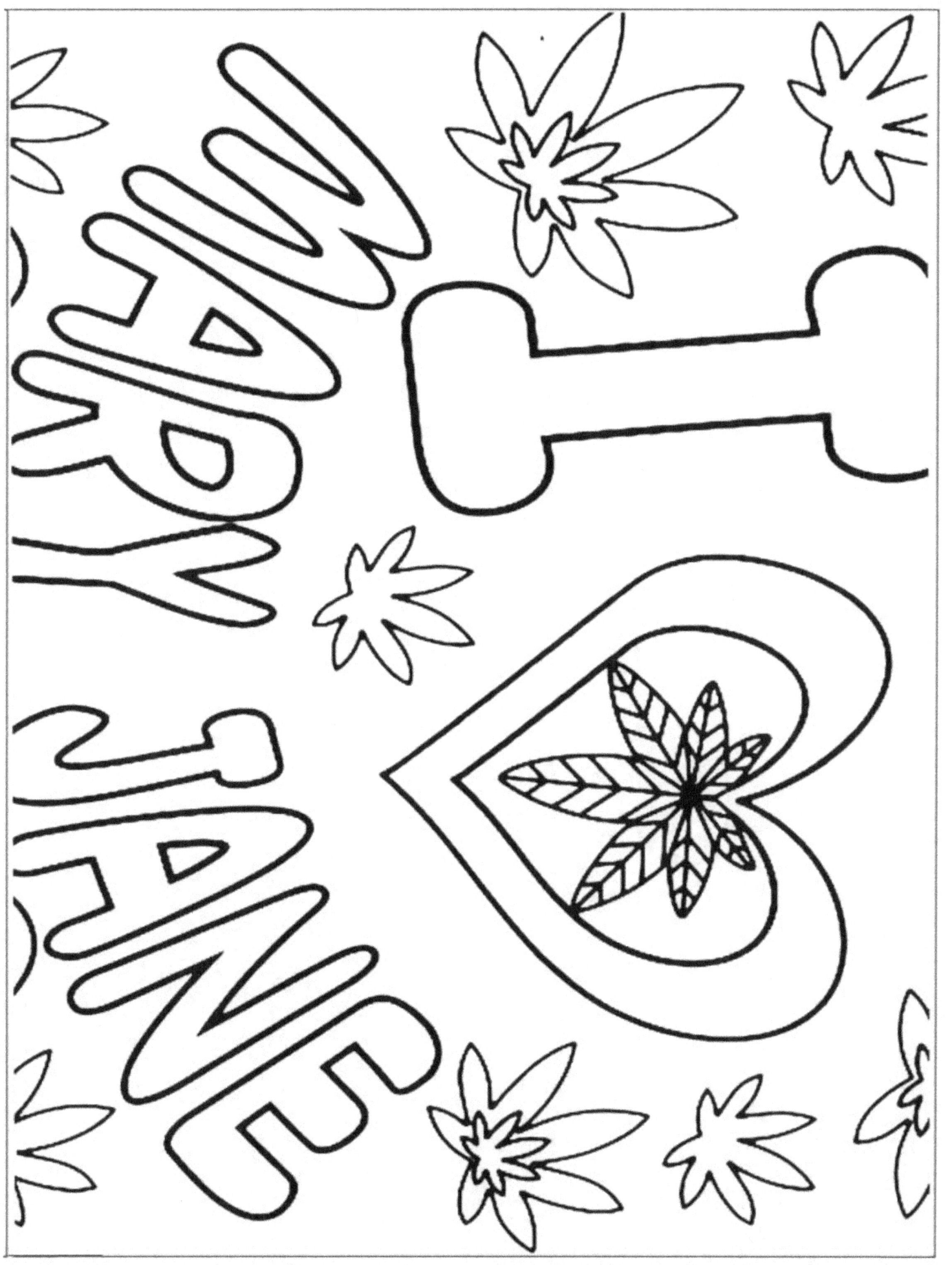

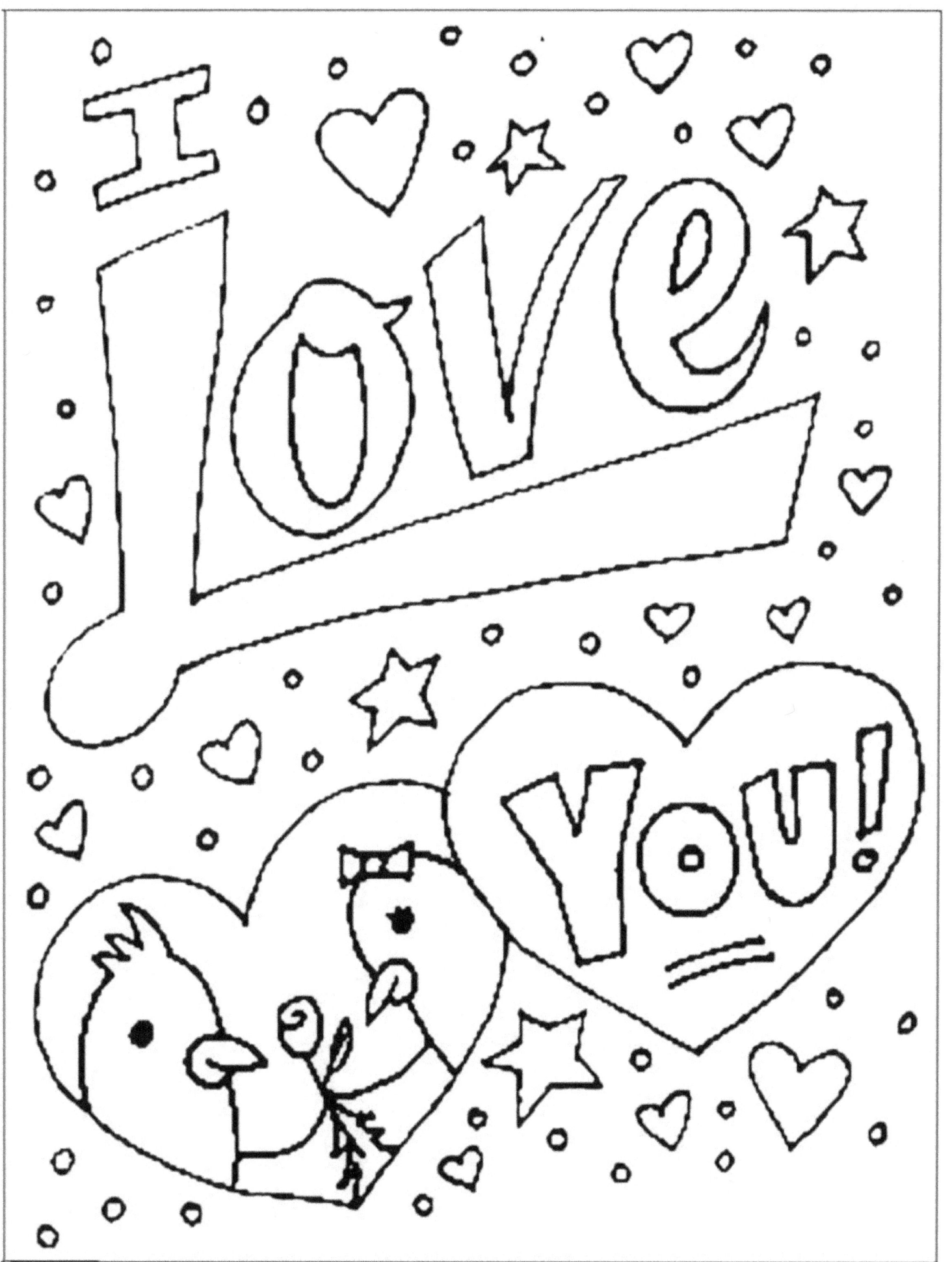

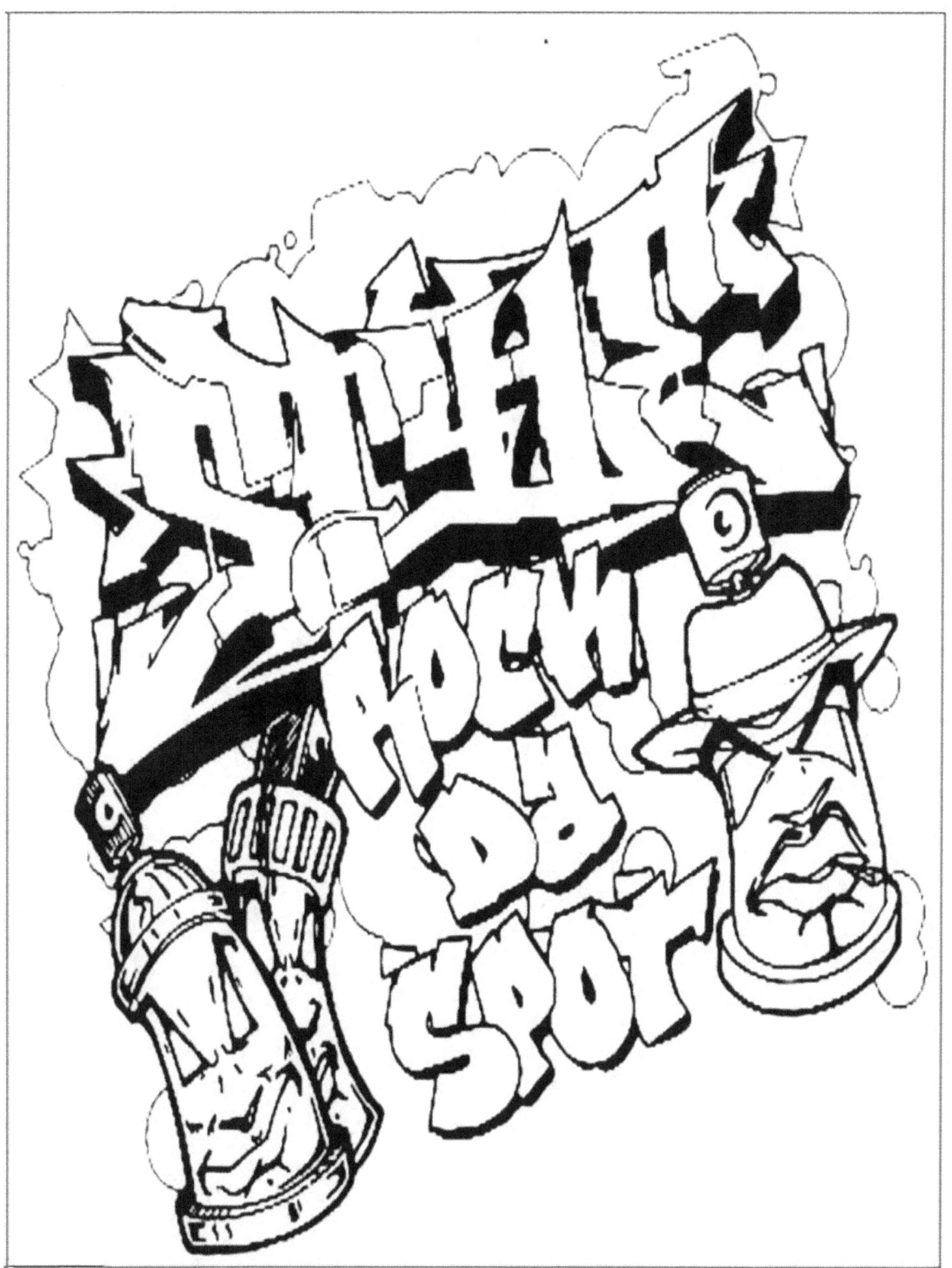

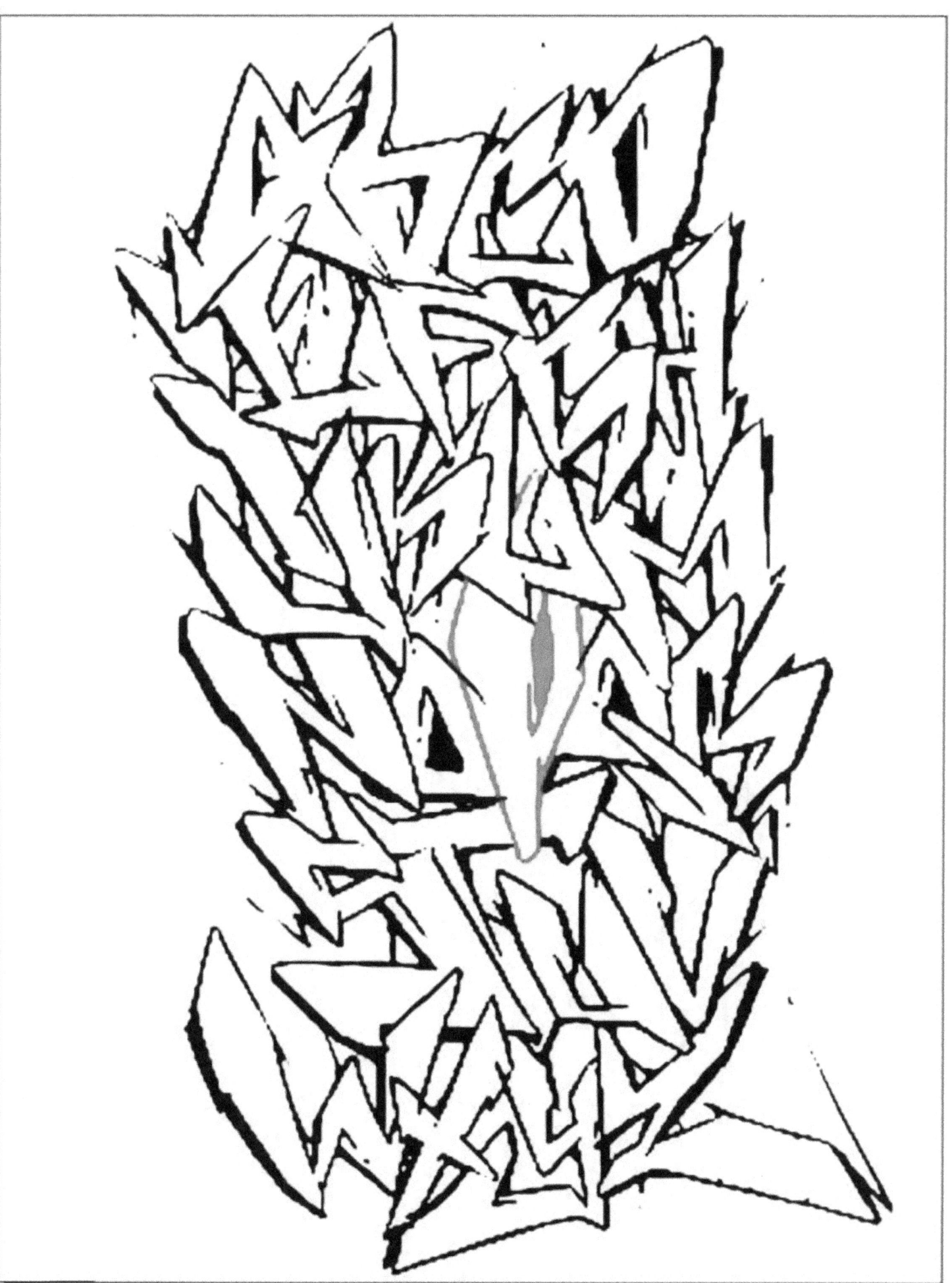

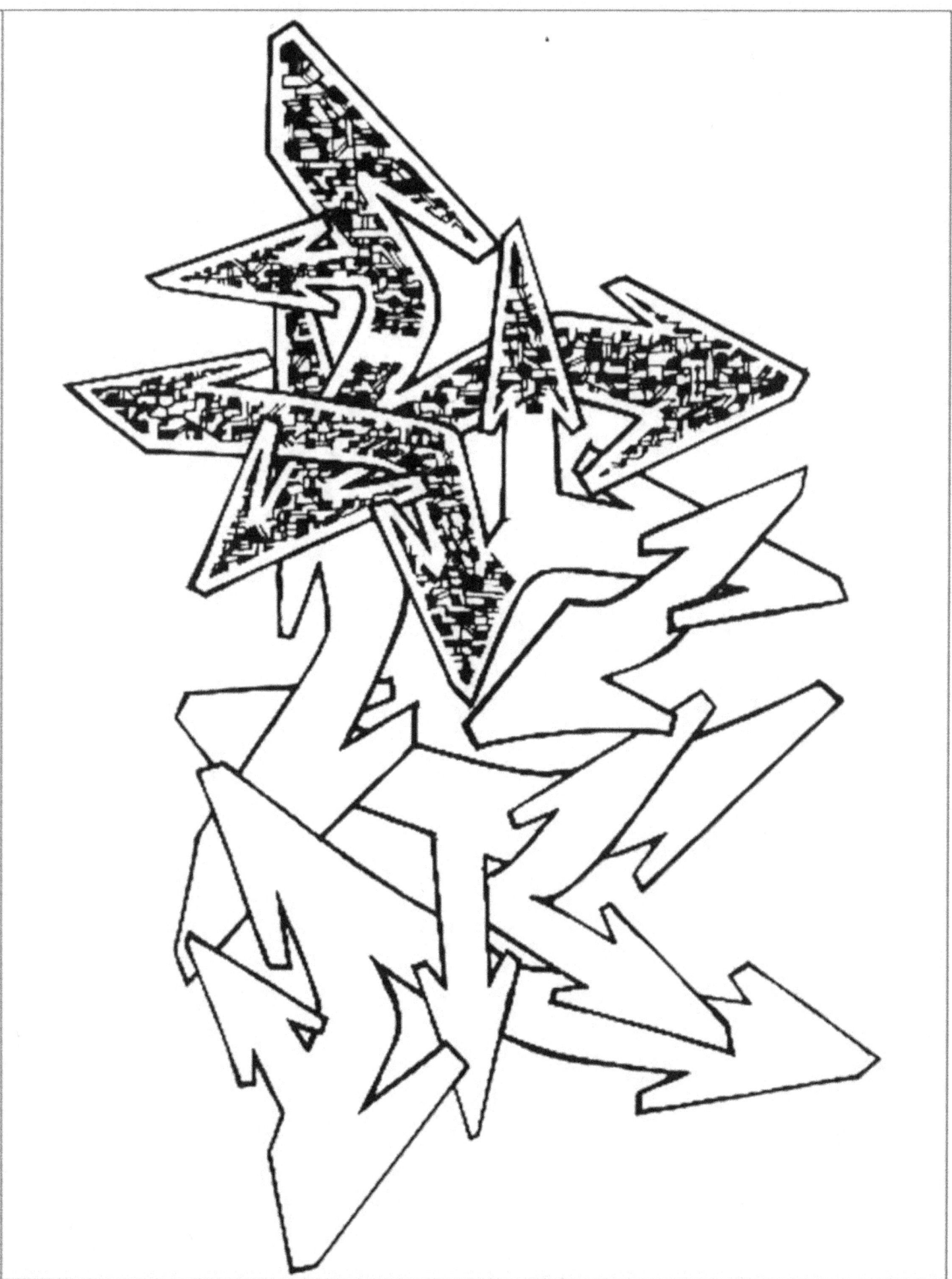

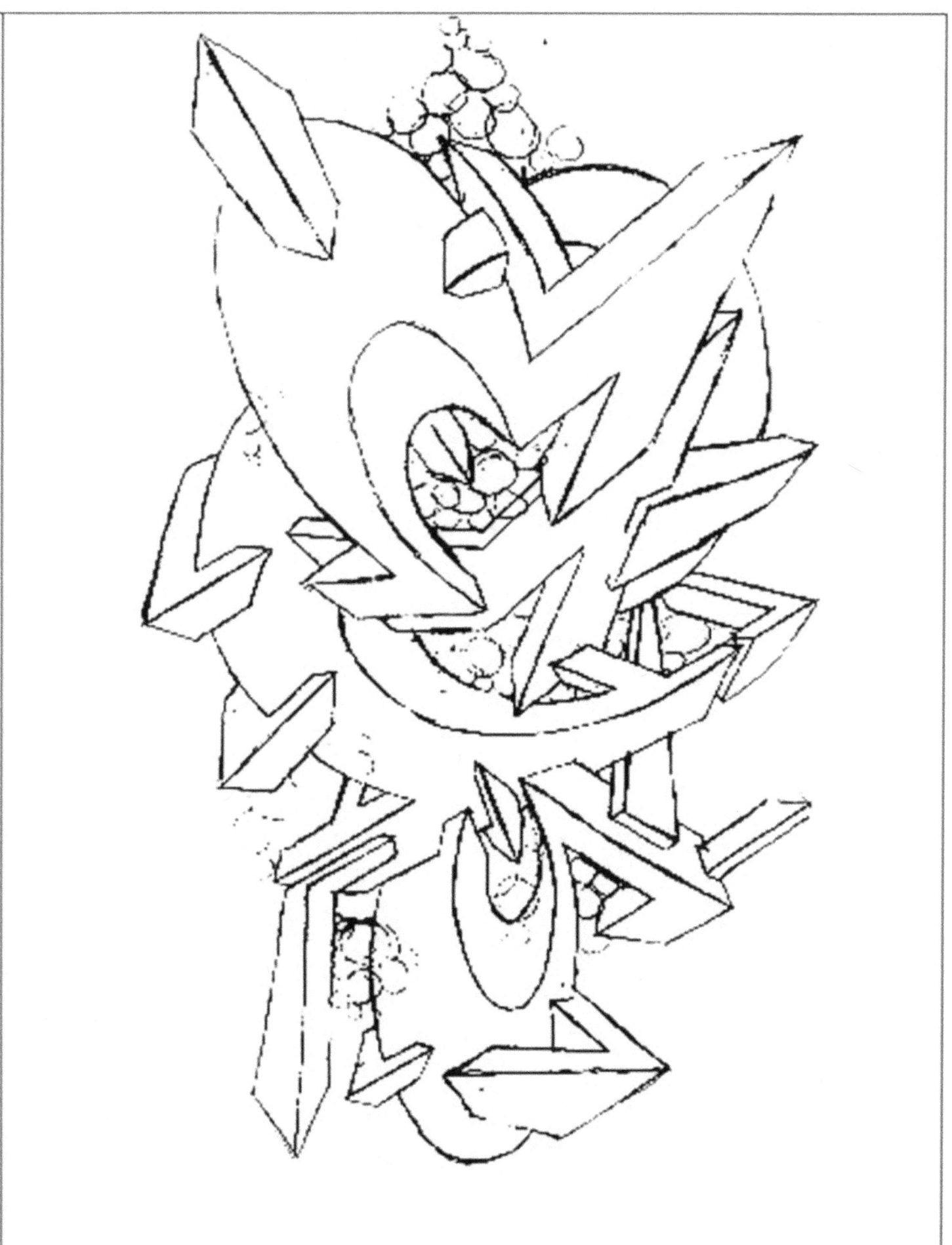

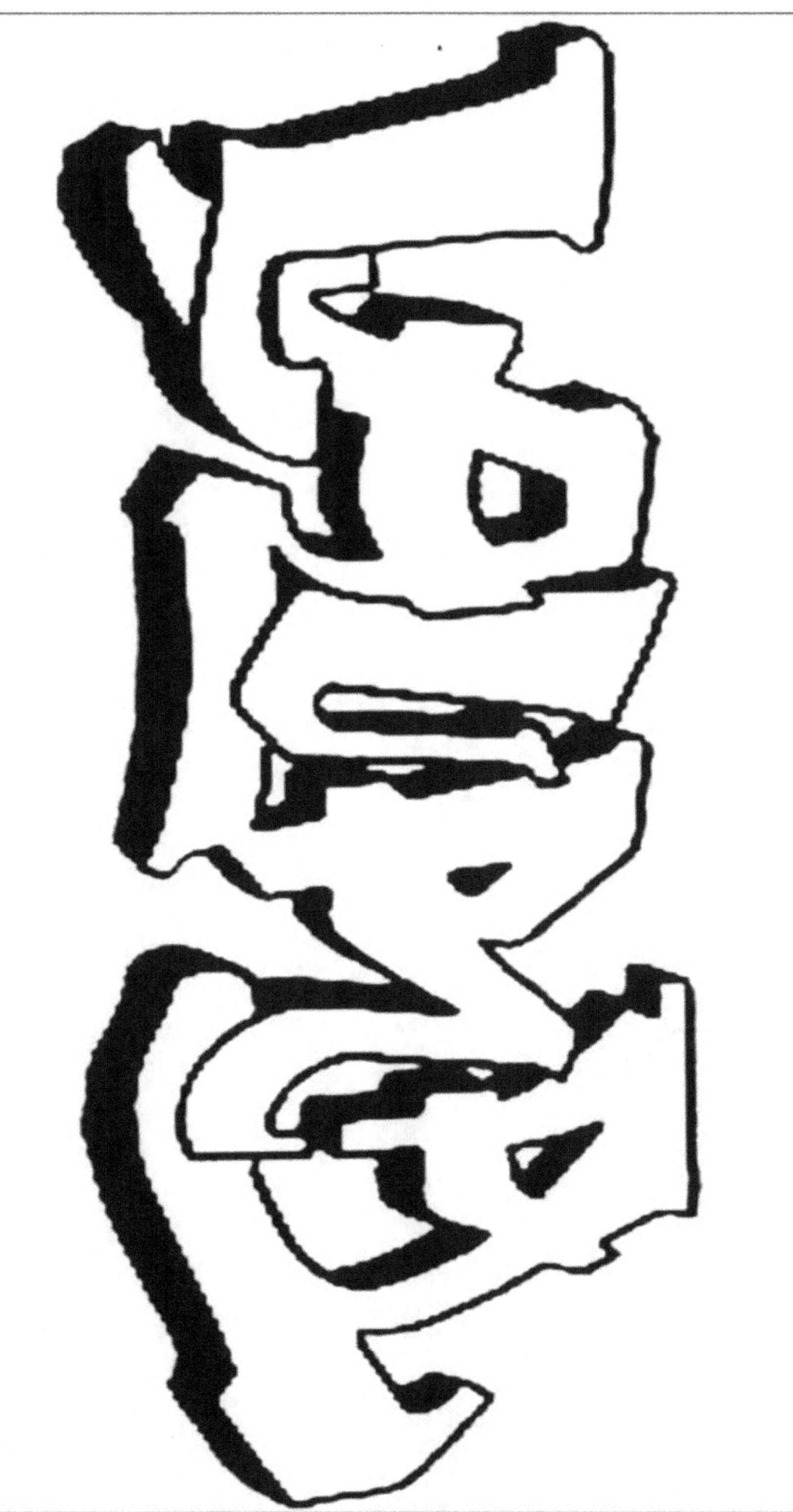

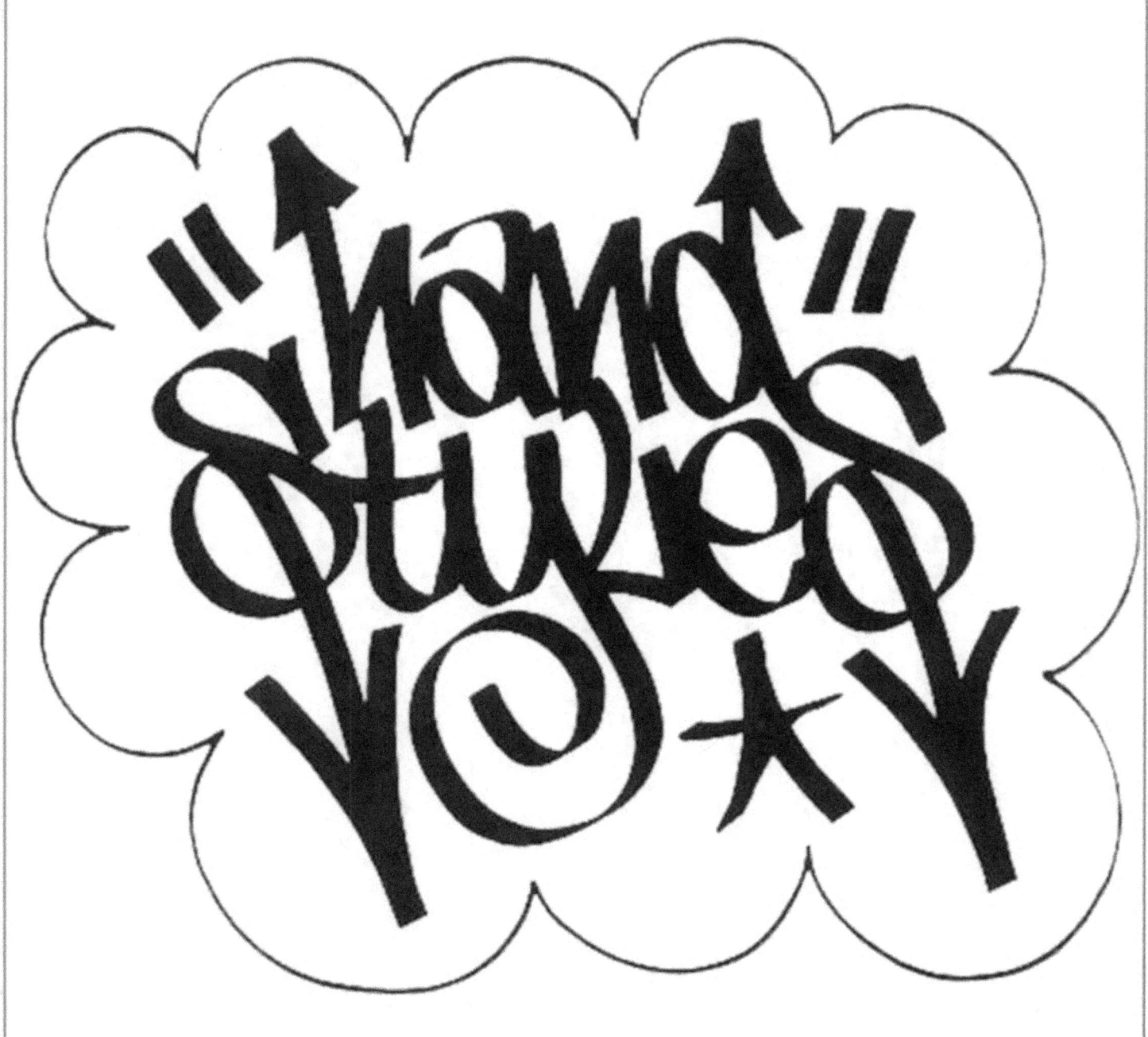

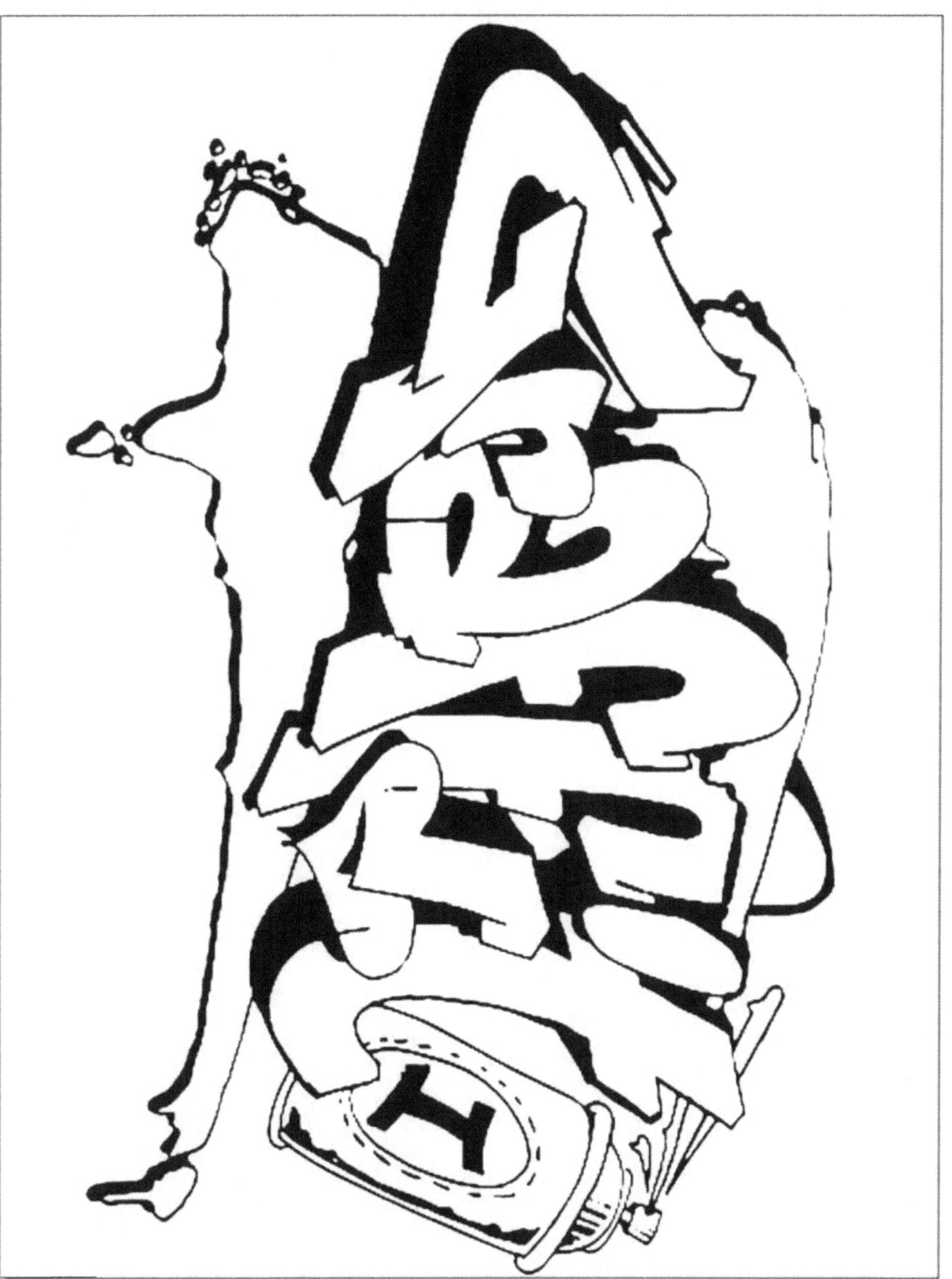

www.ingramcontent.com/pod-product-compliance
Lightning Source LLC
Chambersburg PA
CBHW080951220526
45465CB00008BA/3244